2024 LONGHORN FOOTBALL PROSPECTUS

PROSPECTUS

THINKING TEXAS FOOTBALL

AUTHOR: PAUL WADLINGTON

PHOTOGRAPHER: WILL GALLAGHER

Contents

Greetings!

Welcome to the 12th annual 2024 Longhorn Football Prospectus: Thinking Texas Football. The Burnt Orange Bible is a Texas football preview, a season companion and reference guide, and a resource for the entire 2024 football season.

Thinking Texas Football, in deference to its name, is written for an intelligent football layperson. It won't insult you by writing down to the lowest common denominator nor will it try to overawe you with technical babble. The book's best ambition is to provide you with different tools – while plainly communicating an awareness of its own biases and blind spots – so that we can engage in a conversation that mutually enriches our shared passion.

If you want to see this preview continue to be published and support independent media, please write a 5 star review and share it with your tribe. Word of mouth is our lifeblood and the only way to guarantee future editions.

Hook 'em!

2024 TEXAS: RELOAD OR RETRENCH?

Steve Sarkisian's development trajectory at Texas doesn't require a cryptologist to crack the Enigma Code. The trend is apparent:

2021 - 5-7 (3-6 conference), Unranked, 0 NFL draft picks

2022 - 8-5 (6-3 conference) #25 ranking, 5 NFL draft picks

2023 - 12-2 (8-1 conference) Big 12 champions, Playoffs, #3 ranking, 11 NFL draft picks

Texas' season record has improved by at least three wins every season, the Horns won a conference title and went to the playoffs in Year 3 – just missing a national championship game berth against Michigan – and went from being goose egged in NFL draftable talent to churning out double digit multi-millionaires.

In Sark's 4th year does one just draw the line out on the graph to the clear progression of a 14-1 or 15-0 national title winner? Or do we observe the cautionary wisdom that curves tend to flatten when approaching the top of the y axis? Will Texas continue its meteoric rise, plateau, or reset in a far more competitive league after losing the most NFL talent in school history since the draft went to seven rounds in 1994?

It's possible that Texas improves or maintains their level of play from 2023 qualitatively, but that yields something more like a 11-3 season record in a new league with a challenging non-conference schedule. Qualitatively good football, but a quantitative decline. At least graded by the binary illusion of wins and losses.

Before discussing where Texas is going and where they are, let's talk about where it was. That means briefly revisiting the Big 12. Apply sanitizer liberally, put plastic booties on your shoes and try not to step in anything regrettable. Don't worry, we won't slum it for too long.

One of the defining characteristics of the Big 12 conference in its final years was that its best teams tended to follow a clear developmental cycle – build, climb, peak, decline. After a team reaches its summit, graduation and the NFL draft trigger a rockslide and when the dust clears, they find themselves back at the base of the mountain. Or halfway down and a little disheveled.

The reason for that is simple.

Senior laden teams that lose large numbers to the NFL draft get markedly worse without a massive program talent and developmental feeder to immediately replace, replenish and rejuvenate the two deep. Historically, Big 12 programs – outside of Oklahoma, a flash of Briles' Baylor and peak Texas – simply can't do that. Their process isn't the same as Georgia's.

If you write preview for twelve years, you'll end up with a few regrettable predictions out there in permanent ink, but an understanding of development cycles has served this publication well in fading the dominant teams from prior years that lost lynchpin talent while elevating clear positive trajectory teams on the come up. That's why this preview was so confident in predicting Texas to win the Big 12 last year (accurately projecting a 8-1 conference record, no less) despite widespread cynicism about "same 'ol underachieving Texas" and the legitimate fear that Big 12 referees, at the behest of the petty envy mongers disguised as the league bosses, might see to it that the departing Longhorns would get some inopportune whistles.

That fear was not without some justification. The "impartial" conference commissioner Brett Yormark begged Texas Tech to whip Texas during a preseason Red Raider alumni event and the league's Deputy Director Tim Weiser – who supervises all league officials – resplendent in polyester Men's Wearhouse casual wear, opined sagely at a preseason Big 12 media event that Texas was fleeing the

Big 12 because it would rather lose to Alabama than lose to Kansas State and Iowa State. Throw in every Big 12 football coach mentioning in press conferences that their alums and administration told them that if they won any single game in 2023, it had better be Texas and suddenly it started to feel like Texas may not be in control of its on-field fate in its valedictory Big 12 season. Hands were wrung, lamentations were muttered, pants were peed and Texas fans wondered: Is the fix in?

If this were a Hollywood movie, we would now cut to a summer training montage, season highlights of domination, a flash of scoreboards revealing victory over every remaining Big 12 team and Brett Yormark being lustily booed while handing the Big 12 trophy to a grinning Steve Sarkisian. A scene nearly as satisfying as watching Joey McGuire's Texas Tech bounce an offseason check in Austin that their mouths couldn't cash, only 51 points short of clearing their account in Muleshoe. As for Tim "None the" Weiser and his deep insights into Texas's Jungian motivations for eschewing the league's parasites, Texas whipped Alabama in Tuscaloosa, beat Iowa State in Ames and defeated Kansas State for the 7th year in a row. Texas went out the door as champions, dropping receipts on their opponent's carcasses. That's how you make an exit.

The cycles in the Longhorns' prior league are still instructive and perhaps relevant to Texas still.

Baylor's fade from 12-2 2021 Big 12 champion to 2022's 6-7 disappointment was unsurprising despite the Bears placing 1st in the 2022 Big 12 preseason poll and earning a top 10 preseason national ranking on the strength of their prior year. It's hard for fans and media to conceive that the players – not the helmets, not the uniform, not inherent program winnerness – make the difference. Baylor lost a half dozen key players to the NFL Draft and some extremely valuable free agent super seniors with massive aggregate start numbers. Their dizzying fall from 12-2 to 5-7 to last year's 3-9 proved that 2021 Baylor was a good team, but Dave Aranda never built a good program.

Baylor's 2021 title game opponent, Oklahoma State, saw a similar fall. The Cowboys went from 12-2 and inches from a league title to 7-6 (including a losing conference record) the following season. That disappointing team was picked to finish 12th in the 2022 preseason AP Poll simply because of what had happened in 2021. While their NFL losses were not as dramatic as Baylor, they lost their leading tackler, leading WR, best RB, best blocker and nearly everyone in an excellent secondary. Unsurprisingly, after a one year dip, Mike Gundy brought 2023 Oklahoma State back to the Big 12 championship game. Gundy's ability to belay and arrest his program's falls tells you something about Gundy the program builder.

TCU's obvious fade from the 2022 national title game was also predictable, despite bizarre corporate media projections that had them in every 2023 preseason Top 20. They lost 8 players to the NFL Draft and a number of other free agent super seniors, some of them with as many as 50 career starts. TCU declined from 13-2 to a disappointing 5-7. Their hyped portal class – the media's argument that TCU would circumvent the traditional developmental rhythms of Big 12 programs – merely proved that most highly touted transfers from Bama, LSU and Georgia are transferring for a reason.

So what's the point of all this? Texas isn't a Big 12 team anymore! Is this preview suggesting that Texas is headed for a brutal fall based on NFL Draft losses and tougher competition, just like the teams above?

No, not necessarily.

But we will find out the degree to which Texas is still subject to cyclical ebbs and flows and whether it's still transitioning from a Big 12 program to its new home, or if it's already an SEC blue blood ready to kick ass in a new neighborhood, having taken out the trash in the old one. Notice how many media outlets have already dutifully plugged Texas into 2024's preseason Top 5, despite the Horns losing 11 NFL draft picks. If Sark has created a program, they're right to do so. If 2023 was merely a cyclical apogee, what's the Longhorn floor?

If Texas' DNA is still that of a Big 12 program – subject to build, climb, peak, decline developmental cycles – we'll know it soon enough. If however, Sark has built something different and lasting – a relentless constantly reloading developmental machine consistent with the upper echelons of the SEC – losing eleven athletes to the NFL draft will result not in a pause, but in Next Man Up replenishment, portal domination, SEC title contention, another playoff berth and program dominance.

I like the sound of that.

TWO CONFERENCES MATTER

The prime mover of college football now and into the future is the consolidation of power into just two conferences: the SEC and the Big 10. Within those two leagues the virtuous circle of TV viewership, revenue, talent acquisition and on-field success are mutually reinforcing, multiplicative forces. Each fuels the other and it starts with eyeballs. Because eyeballs mean money.

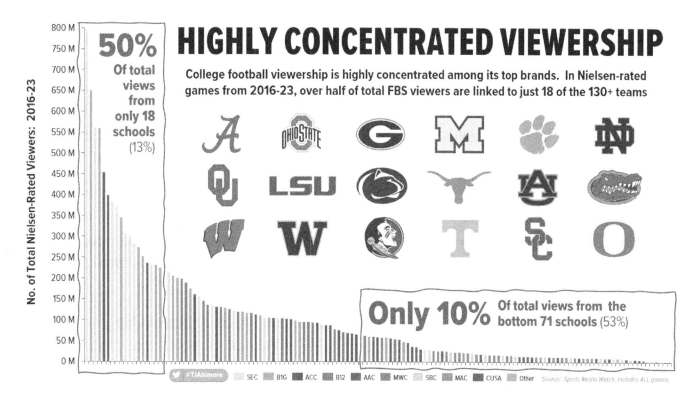

Study the chart above. This is a bit of a self-fulfilling prophecy in that media exposure often goes to winning telegenic teams and winning teams create media exposure. This is also the entire point. However, look closer. There's a message in those metrics about program durability. Winning is less crucial to big loyalty brands than one might imagine. Winning enhances viewership, but what you really want are high floor programs with fervent fan bases that can weather any season.

Losing doesn't necessarily destroy program ratings, does it? These viewership numbers are a program resiliency metric. Texas, Florida, USC, Auburn and Tennessee spent much of 2016-2023 down, but still maintained TV viewership. Throw in facilities, resources, culture, recruiting base, passion and these are elite jobs, even when they're not winning. The prisoners of the moment in college football are always trying to pump up the hot team of that millisecond, but they don't understand the fundamentals. Or the difference between a breakout individual team in a given year and a real program.

Texas was a bad or average football team in six of the eight years studied playing in the worst demographic major conference and still made the Top 10 in viewership. That's extraordinary. Now consider how a weaponized Texas playing good football against a big time SEC schedule with non-conference games against schools like Michigan will fare. Top 5? Top 3? Number 1? We know where the floor is. The ceiling is cavernous.

Washington, Oregon, USC and Wisconsin in that Top 18 should not surprise and all four now share the same league. The Big 10 now defeats every other conference in living alumni and total potential state population draw, but the SEC makes up for it with favorable demographic trends and market intensity. Most importantly, the SEC added Texas. The greatest single prize of all.

The importance of the SEC adding Texas (and in concert with Texas A&M, now fully owning the Texas market) can't be overstated for the league's future. SEC advocates who point to past national titles as evidence of manifest superiority in perpetuity don't understand what adding Texas means for the league's demographic future, particularly vis a vis the Big 10. The state of Texas cements the SEC footprint as the confluence of the greatest natural recruiting base with the best demographic tailwinds: Texas, Tennessee, Florida, South Carolina, Georgia are five of the six fastest growing states in the country. You want to be where people are going, not where they are fleeing from. You want to be where the athletes are grown.

Texas has the second largest state population in the country, but with actual football zeal. California or New York/New Jersey are massive potential markets with questionable goods (football programs) and fewer buyers (viewers). In 2022, 93% of the nation's net native population growth came from Texas, Georgia, North Carolina and Florida. That math is destiny.

15 of the top 18 most watched teams are SEC or Big 10 schools. Texas A&M was 19th. Far from being front-loaded, these leagues are also represented robustly in the next 18 slots – that's Michigan State, Missouri, Iowa, Ole Miss, UCLA, Minnesota, Nebraska, Arkansas, Kentucky, South Carolina. The Big 10 and SEC dominate not just because of their massive roster of elites, but because their so-called "lesser programs" own college football's upper middle class. Each league's teams playing each other creates an accretive growth not reflected in prior numbers. The Big 10 and SEC are growing their pies. Other leagues are fighting for crumbs. This gap will grow, not lessen. It's baked into the arithmetic.

Perhaps the most telling stat on the divide is that the bottom 71 teams account for only 10% of all viewership. This is Pareto's Principle on PEDs. That's during a time period when less represented schools have the most exposure in college football history due to mid-week games and a profusion of sports channels. That is bad news for the ACC and Big 12. Without getting too mired in the details, Big 12 games with Texas or Oklahoma routinely drew 3x to 5x of what league games without them did. It's clear who was propping up the league and it wasn't TCU-Cincinnati.

There are now only two major conferences and a small handful of one-off individual programs that matter. And the one-offs are all fighting to get into The Two That Matter (see myriad ACC lawsuits). That gap is expanding, not narrowing.

Let's throw out the television money and revenues for a moment. It's not as if Texas fans get cheaper tickets or reduced Longhorn Foundation donor obligations because Texas Inc is printing money like the Federal Reserve. Football purists want to see the best football possible. What about talent on the field? Well, look at the on-field results. Since 2000, the current Big 10 or SEC has won every national title except for three. Those three? Two titles by Clemson and one by Florida State; and both schools are vying to join the two aforementioned leagues.

There is another measure of talent output and it is pretty objective. It's called the NFL Draft. Let's take the 2024 draft and sort it by the new conference alignments. Who is churning out the best players and thus attracting the most elite recruits with ambitions for Sundays?

THE 2024 POST REALIGNMENT DRAFT

Conference	Total Draftees	Per Team Average
SEC	73	(4.5)
B10	69	(3.8)
ACC	43	(2.5)
B12	26	(1.6)

The SEC wins over the Big 10 narrowly in volume and meaningfully in quality. The Big 10 is the clear #2, but the gap in quality between the Big 10 and ACC is almost twice the gap between the SEC and Big 10. 67% of the draftable Power 4 talent came from only two leagues: the SEC and Big 10. The Big 12 is going to be a highly competitive and balanced league, but so is the MAC. Its talent output will be closer to the MAC than the SEC. That does not mean they won't play entertaining football. But the gap in talent and revenues will increase and the interaction between the two reinforces the growth of the other.

One year is not exactly robust data. However, that is the new landscape. The chasm between the SEC to the other two conferences might as well be the Grand Canyon. A Grand Canyon that adds a hundred feet of width and depth a year. Now consider the future guarantee of the ACC's elites leaving. FSU and Clemson were responsible for 37.2% of the ACC's 2024 draft class. Without those two schools, the ACC has as many draft picks as the Big 12.

Arguing about the 3rd best league is like arguing about the 3rd best member of Van Halen. There may be a right answer, but who cares once you get past Eddie and Diamond Dave? Any discussions of the Power 4 shaping college football beyond the SEC and Big 10 and a handful of other individual one-off programs (Notre Dame, Florida State, Clemson), demonstrates a lack of understanding of the political, fiscal or competitive realities that now exist and will only accelerate over time. Additionally, the flow of the elites in the transfer portal will inordinately go from the FCS/Group of 5 to Power 4, while also flowing from the P Bottom (B12, ACC) to the P Elite (SEC, B10). The SEC and Big 10 will start to treat their subordinates as farm systems. The ACC and Big 12 also share the misfortune of having considerable geographic overlap with the SEC and Big 10 powers, so they can't even appeal to regionalism or state pride to stave off the more powerful leagues.

What about the non Power Four's 2024 NFL Draft?

Independent	**8**
Sun Belt	**6**
American	**5**
Conference USA	**3**
Mountain West	**2**
MAC	**2**

Note that the G5 leagues (Sun Belt, American, CUSA, Mountain West, MAC) combined for 18 picks. Independents Notre Dame and UConn combined for 8.

Why is that important?

Because in 2019, there were 36 G5 draft picks. The Mountain West had 10 by itself. The portal funnel for elite talent runs in one direction. Their stars are transferring out and up. Additionally, the FCS (schools like Montana, South Dakota State, Samford etc) had 20 total NFL draft picks in 2022. This year? 11. Care to guess what that number will look like in 2027? Late bloomers and high performing under-the-radar types are being vacuumed up by the money leagues.

What about high school recruiting? What two leagues offer credible evidence that they are the truest NFL Developmental Leagues with the most intensity of interest, best NIL, national television span, elite facilities, scale?

Every future trend line points in only one direction.

There are now two leagues that matter. Texas is in one of them because of the leadership of men like Kevin Eltife and Jay Hartzell. Two Conferences Matter is not a statement of aspiration or even satisfaction. The final consolidation of power in the college landscape ends a long great regional chapter in the history of college football that many will and perhaps should mourn. I attach as much emotion to the analysis as I do stating that the law of gravity exists. It simply is. Our feelings about falling out of a window don't really factor into the fall. So Texas can set a bold course and lead one of the leagues that matter or we can flap our arms like a Looney Tunes character who ran off of a cliff and hope that physics don't apply.

Texas made the right choice.

QUARTERBACK

Player	Height	Weight	Class
Quinn Ewers	6'2"	210	JR
Arch Manning	6'4"	225	FR/RS
Cole Lourd	6'2"	215	SR
Joe Tatum	5'11"	185	JR

Quinn Ewers decided to devote himself more seriously to his craft after an up and down first year as a starter by focusing on better nutrition, determined S&C and more intensive film study. Ewers cut his trademark mullet to signal a more businesslike approach and worked to get into the best shape of his life. Those efforts yielded a 25 pound weight loss, better mobility, increased comfort in the offense and more attention to detail. Additional modifications like choosing to play in cleats rather than crocs and in football pants in lieu of jean shorts were not just aesthetic. Switching out in-game hydration from single grain scotch and Mountain Dew to the more conventional choice of water may have yielded additional benefits, but the science is inconclusive. Whether his old habit of firing Costco spray cheese directly into his mouth for post workout recovery is superior to his current menu of lean protein, creatine and vegetables is indeterminate. Is panic-swallowing Copenhagen during a blitz really that bad for you? No one knows. Ultimately, these are theological questions.

The point is that Cleaned Up Quinn is here to stay and it has yielded a better quarterback, even if we all secretly loved having an offensive leader that could toss touchdowns with an ashy Marlboro Red hanging loosely from his mouth like a young Steve McQueen.

Yes, Ewers' offseason cleanup last year has been a little overdone by the media and I'm having some fun with it, but it's also clear that a young athlete rethought his image and role and made changes that yielded considerable improvements in his play. That's in addition to the natural progression that any first year signal caller would have accrued playing for Sark and position coach AJ Milwee with an additional another year of development. Last season, Ewers improved considerably in every discernible metric.

The raw numbers speak volumes: Ewers completed 272 of 394 attempts for 3,479 yards, 22 touchdowns and only 6 interceptions. Ewers went from an above average 132.6 pass efficiency rating in 2022 to a strong 158.6 in 2023 and ballooned his average yards per attempt from a middling 7.4 to a very robust 8.8. His completion percentage also blossomed from 58.1% to 69.0% and he completed less than 63% of his passes only twice during the 2023 season. Ewers would have had a real shot at breaking 4,000 passing yards if he hadn't missed two games. Quinn continues to take good care of the ball (the nearly obligatory media description of him as "a gunslinger" doesn't mirror his actual style of play) and his 12 career interceptions in 690 attempts means that he throws an interception a mere 1.7% of the time when the ball leaves his hand. If that holds, he will edge out Sam Ehlinger as the least intercepted QB in Longhorn history. With a full 2024 season, Ewers should finish his career as the third most prolific passer in Texas history behind Colt McCoy and Ehlinger.

Ewers also discovered better mobility, moving from a 24 rush, -52 yard performance as a redshirt freshman to a 59 carry, 75 yards and 5 touchdown effort last year. No one will confuse him with one Vincent Paul Young carrying the rock, but that represents a major shift in productivity. Since the college game adds sacks to a quarterback's rushing totals, neither number may impress but Ewers moved better in the pocket and showed himself capable of punishing defenses with a well-timed scamper when they turned their back on him in man coverage. He amassed 54 yards on 8 carries against Washington and added a 29 yard touchdown run against Baylor where he actually looked fast.

While weight loss certainly benefited his mobility and footwork, he neglected lifting weights and that loss of strength – particularly in the lower body – made him less resilient in the pocket. He couldn't shrug off hands and glancing blows, his base depleted and there were times that he wilted in the pocket (a 51.5% completion rate when pressured) rather than stand strong and deliver the ball. He spent the offseason gaining back good weight (he is up about 17 pounds and stronger) and that will help him in standing firmer against the rush, keeping his eyes up and not succumbing to mild to moderate contact.

One of the most interesting things about Ewers is how contextual his passing strengths and weaknesses are. In his wheelhouse, he's outstanding. Outside of it, something less than that. Consider passing depth of target efficiency:

Distance	Att/Comp/Yds	TD/INT	Comp. %	YPA
20+ yards	47/16/580 yards	4 td/ 1 int	34% comp	12.3
10-19 yards	105/72/1326 yards	10 td/ 2 int	68.6% comp	12.6
0-9 yards	109/81/746 yards	6 td/ 3 int	74.3% comp	6.8
Behind LOS	106/101/808 yards	2 td/ 0 int	95.3% comp	7.6

Ewers was vastly improved but still too inaccurate on deep balls, completing only 34% of his attempts. However, those he connected on went for 36.3 yards per catch and those completions scored touchdowns 25% of the time. 12.3 yards per deep ball attempt is good and a massive improvement over last year's 7.9, but Ewers' problem remains inconsistency and that's how it felt during games: his deep balls hit a bit too infrequently, but when they did, the defense paid the price. If #3 can get up to a 50% completion mark on five or six deep balls per game, the Longhorn offense will be terrifying.

Ewers sparkled as an intermediate thrower (10-19 yards), racking up an impressive 12.6 yards per attempt and 18.4 yards per completion. This is where he did the most efficient damage as a passer with the most reliable consistency. The eye test agrees with the data. Quinn's best big time throws were frequently intermediate dimes on difficult routes or layered drops between three defenders that yielded additional yards after catch. Quinn is truly special on these often nuanced throws and it's always affirming when the data crunching and game watch agree.

Ewers is also terrific throwing at or behind the line of scrimmage. That is not damning with faint praise. Swings and screens dominate this area of the field and accurate ball placement is key for maximization. The difference between perfectly leading a receiver on the upfield shoulder to the correct hand at numbers height with catchable zip versus fluttering a screwball off-time just behind them is the difference between an 11 yard gain and a 2 yard loss. Yes, these are short passes, but many still travel 20 yards in the air and require real precision. Not only did Ewers complete a sizzling 95% of his attempts, but his ball placement maximized these de facto runs of the passing game, yielding a healthy 7.6 yards per attempt. For that part of the field, that's quality stuff. A 8 yard gain with a 95% likelihood? Yeah, we'll probably take that.

So where did Ewers struggle most *on an efficiency basis*? Not the deep ball, actually. It was on throws between 0-9 yards. Surprised? Me too. Until I reviewed the season film again. It checks out. He completed these throws 74% of the time and they didn't go for much (6.8 yards per attempt, 9.2 yards per completion). This area of the field is where he also had his worst touchdown:interception ratio: 6 to 3. On all other throws, he managed 16 touchdowns to 3 picks. This is the average depth of target where Ewers threw the most, so improvements here would have a meaningful impact on overall team efficiency. These routes are classic chain movers: slants, quick outs, stops, short crossers, blitz beaters and checkdowns.

Some of these routes put a cap on yards after catch by their very nature, but almost every meaningful metric in this subset for Ewers is an outlier vis a vis other high profile quarterbacks...in a negative way. Georgia's Carson Beck hit 85% of these throws at 7.5 yards per attempt. Colorado's Shedeur Sanders hit 84% at 7.6 yards per attempt. Alabama's Jalen Milroe completed 86% at 8.0 yards per attempt. Collectively, those three also had a 21 touchdown to 2 interception ratio in this passing range, in contrast to Ewers at 6 to 3. If Ewers progressed to a 85% completion benchmark at this average depth of target, it would result in a dozen more completions, a couple of additional touchdowns, a couple less interceptions and another half dozen 3rd down conversions.

These shorter routes seem to bear some similarity to his deep balls in that he doesn't have a consistently replicable set of mechanics to nail them down, whereas his passing behind the LOS is almost flawless and his sheer playmaking on intermediate balls is elite. Could it be as simple as not having developed a really consistent and repeatable throwing style and rhythm that only reveals itself on certain throws? Are these throws more revealing of consistent mechanics than arm talent?

Part of what made Ewers beguiling as a recruit was his knack for releasing the ball accurately from a dizzying variety of arm angles and different platforms. The downside of that is that Ewers never developed a base throwing motion that he could fall back on when he just needs to deliver the correct ball on time in rhythm with the offense. He can drill a 25 foot off balance 3 pointer, but then miss two free throws. That lack of a duplicable platform particularly plagues quarterbacks on certain set piece throws that are mainstays in any offense. Deep post. Short stop or slant. Go route. These routes don't require "arm talent" per se. Just touch, rhythm and ball placement. They are not lay-ups, but they are free throws. And anyone can become a good free throw shooter if they develop replicable mechanics and practice.

Conversely, watching an arm talent deficient touch and rhythm quarterback try to nail a 15 yard out or a 20 yard deep comeback is painful. Ewers can hit those throws looking bored while stifling a yawn, throwing off of his back foot with the ball hovering around his hip before the release.

While we're slaying myths, Ewers has a reputation amongst the casual fans as a pure spread QB who thrives when you spread it out to four or five wide and let it fly. The data tells a different story. On play action throws – both traditional play action and RPOs – Ewers completed 75% of his passes at 10 yards per attempt. Outstanding. Most dangerous Quinn is the play action Quinn. While play action can be run from any formation that isn't an empty set, Texas chooses to run play action almost exclusively from two and three WR sets, not four wide. Ewers' best throws come via play action out of distinct personnel groupings to specific areas of the field. He's arguably the best passer in college football when his attempt is paired with a convincing ball fake and the offensive line influences accordingly. Without play action? Ewers averages a ho-hum 7.4 yards per attempt and completes 61% of his balls.

Does defensive philosophy impact Ewers as well? Absolutely. It's less about coverages and more about pressure – real or perceived. Ewers saw a significant performance decline when blitzed. When blitzed, he averaged only 7.1 yards per attempt and completed 64% of his balls. When not blitzed, he completed a razor sharp 71% of his throws and a dangerous 9.7 yards per attempt. Being blitzed is not the same as being pressured – all QBs tend to fall off of an efficiency cliff when they're moved off of their spot and hit hard – but most blitzes don't make it to the QB. Even an unsuccessful blitz will speed up the internal clock and is more likely to force Ewers into many of his least efficient throws between 0-9 yards or a less probable deep ball, too often thrown off balance or from a shoddy platform. Given that the two most frequent responses to a blitz are either a deep ball or a quick route to a receiver at 0-9 yards depth, there is a clear interrelation between blitzing and Ewers' depth of target struggles. This is useful information for anyone scouting Texas, but fortunately this book self-destructs if touched by any Texas opponent.

Caution: it can be dangerous to attribute everything to the quarterback when it may simply be an inherent part of the offensive structure or reflective of the skills and weaknesses of the skill players around them, but these are data worth internalizing and watching for as the season progresses. If Ewers and the offense show improvement in some of these key performance indicators, the analysis that "Ewers and the receivers are good and Sark is dialing up good plays so the Texas offense plays good" may be accurate, but not very instructive as to why. Perhaps the most interesting development of the offseason will be whether Ewers can develop a core foundational throwing motion that he can improvise off of, rather than making the improvisation itself his foundation. Move that free throw shooting percentage from 70% to 85%. If he does that – with tangible improvement throwing at distances 0-9 yards and more consistent link ups at 20+ yards – Texas will have an even more dangerous offense despite losing no less than six NFL draft picks from the offense. Ewers will also certainly hear his own name called in the first round at season's end and leave Texas with 30+ lifetime wins at QB.

Arch Manning occupies an enviable space at Texas. First, he's a blue chip backup QB, which makes him the most popular and blameless player on the team. All of his positive traits are celebrated and a lack of game day action means that he has no revealed faults. Second, he's clan Manning: actual American football royalty. Not the annoying, attention-seeking Prince Harry and Meghan kind of royalty. More like an actual family of cool people that are really damn good at throwing footballs. Third, beyond the hype, he might actually be good. Like, really, really good.

Arch had an impressive coming out party in the Spring game with an ensuing whirlwind of positive media attention – a stark contrast to last year's "Derrrrr, He's A Bust!" proclamations from predictable idiots after Sark surrounded him with backup offensive linemen and walk-ons. It was a good way of shielding Manning from expectations and a fine example that beneath the laid back, California cool facade, Sark is old school and thinks it's a useful rite of passage to make young players suffer and adapt. A year later, Manning made the Texas defense suffer and looked like a completely different player. The young passer completed 19 of 26 passes for 355 yards while tossing three touchdowns. Beyond the raw numbers and production, how he did it looked even more impressive. His level of refinement relative to his age and inexperience is difficult to overstate. As a redshirt freshman, he's already demonstrating the athleticism of his father Cooper (a college level wide receiver whose career was sidelined by injury) and Grandpa Archie, the consistent throwing platform of Uncle Eli and the field awareness of Uncle Peyton. No one knows if he can cook like grandma Olivia. This preview isn't that good.

Rapid pocket resets tied to active eyes that remain fixed downfield, speedy progressions plus sterling mechanics featuring a duplicable, compact delivery means that he can make the tough throws, but can also reliably drill the ample free throws and lay-ups that Sark's offense provides. Arch's footwork, posture and ball position allow a trigger pull the moment it touches his hands. That means he's always ready to throw and windows don't pass him by. Manning's compact, efficient delivery and properly spaced footwork allows constant resets in the pocket without losing trigger potential. He's already developing an NFL level understanding that shifting six inches and taking a small step forward can transform a withering pass rush into a mild inconvenience.

Beyond his accuracy and considerable intangibles, Manning is a big athletic passer with a very strong lower body. Manning's speed and physicality is the least discussed part of his game, but it offers the tantalizing prospect of a high level point guard of on-schedule offense who distributes assists but can also rumble for 30 yards against man coverage on 3rd and 4 or shake off a pass rusher and buy the extra second needed to spring a big gain downfield.

Coaches and program observers are impressed with his humble demeanor, football IQ and competitiveness. The less informed who thought that Manning might transfer because Ewers returned for his junior season are missing the plot and don't understand the protagonists of the tale. The Mannings aren't live-through-the-athlete parasites or street agents looking for a quick payout. They want Arch to have an actual college experience, develop on an appropriate timeline, to socialize as a young man and (gasp) get an education. They are media and football sophisticated and understand that pressing Arch into early action in Austin or elsewhere to satisfy idiotic media demands or the expectations of strangers they've never met is ruinous to his development. Manning doesn't need to start for three years to go to the NFL. However, if pressed to start this year, the Texas offense will be just fine.

Trey Owens had a fine Spring showing of his own. The big passer from Cy-Fair went 14 of 21 for 228 yards and 3 touchdowns. He threw several dimes, he threw a few pennies and he threw a couple he'd like back in the piggy bank, but there's much to like about the 6'5[2033?] freshman who played with his seat belt unbuckled for four quarters. From a developmental perspective, I'm reminded that Patrick Mahomes will be the ruin of young quarterbacks everywhere. Trey throws with a varying sidearm 3/4 delivery. It makes him throw like he's 6'2[2033?], not 6'5[2033?], and it elongates everything he does. It also prevents him from firing through flash windows and pocket clutter can disrupt him. To enable that delivery, he often holds the ball at his stomach and then winds out and back before release. Telegraphed and the ball gets out more slowly. Still, mechanical tweaks are to be expected for a young passer. The more important takeaway is that the true freshman was utterly fearless under bright lights and he has real ability paired with a huge frame. Big body quarterbacks who show no fear and can place a ball like a faberge egg in a cotton-filled shoebox thirty yards downfield are always welcome.

Cole Lourd rounds out the embarrassment of riches at QB. While Lourd may be 3rd or 4th string, he's a capable passer who looks like he could easily contend for a starting job at many Group of Five schools. The fourth year senior knows the system well and could be a live option if the unthinkable ever happened. Pray that our Lourd and savior is not needed.

Prognosis

Football is a violent game and the expectation that a starting quarterback could miss a game or three is not improbable bad luck, but a reasonable likelihood. Indeed, Quinn Ewers has missed 5 starts over the last two years despite no lack of toughness and grit and he has played through injury in a handful of other contests. Hope for the best, but prepare for the worst. Fortunately for Texas, few teams can boast an insurance policy as impressive as Arch Manning.

Quinn Ewers should at least match his improved level of play from last year, but in his 3rd year in Sark's system, playing behind a quality pass blocking offensive line, throwing to top 10% FBS skill players, with plays designed and called by one of the best offensive architect's in the country, it's every bit as likely that he will continue to grow rather than just plateau. As outlined in his player profile, if he can double down on his strengths and expand some of his competencies, the number of college teams boasting equivalent passing games can be counted on one hand. Expect the Horns to throw it around the yard pretty well this year.

RUNNING BACK

Player	Height	Weight	Class
CJ Baxter	6'1"	220	SO
Jaydon Blue	6'0"	200	JR
Quintrevion Wisner	6'0"	200	SO
Christian Clark	6'0"	210	FR
Jerrick Gibson	5'10"	205	FR
Colin Page	6'0"	210	JR

Jaydon Blue had a tantalizing 2023 despite seeing limited action for most of the year behind star running back Jonathon Brooks and freshman CJ Baxter. A season-ending injury to Brooks and the desire to get Blue's speed on the field earned Jaydon increased snaps late in the season and he responded with 398 rushing yards at 6.1 yards per carry and 14 catches for 135 yards while totaling 4 touchdowns. Longhorns fans were left wanting more. A collective case of....Blue balls?

Last year was the prologue to what should be Blue's 2024 breakout.

Blue is one of the fastest players in college football (he was clocked at 22.3 mph on his 69 yard touchdown run against Texas Tech) and he pairs that with elusiveness and ever improving physicality between the tackles. Jaydon has also broken the speedster's bad habit of trying to break everything outside and now understands that one cut and go, up the field, shoulders squared, is how most big runs are created.

In the playoff game against Washington, Blue ran for 59 yards on only 9 carries and was seemingly in the groove on the way to a triple digit yardage effort until a critical 3rd quarter fumble on a checkdown pass derailed Longhorn momentum. Ball security must improve for Blue to reach his full potential and earn the workload that he deserves. Blue had an outstanding Spring game and his effortless 29 yard catch and run touchdown from Arch Manning highlighted his continued evolution as a complete running back. Equally impressive was a no-nonsense 3rd and short conversion where Blue lowered his pads and burrowed for a hard three yards. Now a junior, Blue is stronger, more mature and expects this to be a contract year. While comparisons to former Bama and current Detroit Lion standout Jahmyr Gibbs are bold, you don't have to squint much to see it. The shocking quickness and combo threat as a runner and receiver are evident. National attention and corporate preseason guide focus remains on the recruiting pedigree of his backfield mate, but Blue is the most dangerous runner in the Longhorn stable and one of the most devastating big play weapons on the roster.

CJ Baxter saw quite a bit of action in his rookie season and the former #1 running back prospect in the nation showed promise while also demonstrating that he is far from a finished product. Production, toughness and assignment maturity were on point, but individual run maximization was not. Last season, Baxter rarely added supplementary yards to a well-blocked play and far too many of his runs ended at first contact. Baxter totaled 659 yards rushing and caught 24 balls out of the backfield, but his 4.8 yards per carry average and 6.5 yards per catch reception average made him an outlier compared to Brooks and Blue (both averaged 6.1 yards per carry and a combined 10.8 yards per catch). Injuries plagued Baxter throughout the season and he had to work through nagging foot, rib and hip injuries all year. To his credit, he fought through a lot of pain and discomfort and exhibited unexpected maturity as a selfless pass protector.

The lack of run maximization and soft tissue injuries share a common origin. Baxter arrived at Texas less physically developed than most big backs. Most elite backs are early bloomers, but Baxter has still yet to fully blossom. For runners, adding muscle and good weight doesn't just enable power and tackle breaking. It's armor. An actual protective mechanism. CJ also frequently ran with too upright a pad level and that's particularly dangerous for backs over 6 feet tall. That frame already presents a big target for tacklers between the knees and numbers and those are the places where hard hits turn to nagging soft tissue injuries that compound over time. Baxter is still learning to "get small" at contact and continue driving through it with violence. Spring revealed a stronger runner with better pad level who can better break tackles. If that persists and he can continue to add good weight and strength this summer, Texas will have a formidable 1-2 punch in the Blue & Baxter combo.

Tre Wisner is a selfless player that coaches rave about for his effort and mature approach. Though he only managed 12 carries last year as a 4th string true freshman backup at a crowded position, Wisner made a name for himself as a special teams maniac (7 tackles on kick coverage, including a couple of detonations of enemy kick returners) and endeared himself to coaches and teammates with effort and surprising physicality for a player who was billed out of high school as a speedy finesse back who might even end up in the slot one day. Wisner is equally comfortable as a receiver or runner and a solid offseason weight gain up to 200 pounds will only help his cause in earning reps along with Blue and Baxter.

Christian Clark and **Jerrick Gibson** are true freshmen who may have an opportunity to assert themselves if Tashard Choice likes the dimension(s) that they add. Gibson is a no frills punishing grinder with a penchant for falling forward while Clark is more of a slasher with the frame to add more weight and explosive power.

Prognosis

Before last season, Texas fans wondered who could adequately replace beloved departed runners Bijan Robinson and Roschon Johnson, but Jonathon Brooks showed out brilliantly as the Longhorns' bell cow and as a backfield receiver. Sadly, his season ended after ten games with a knee injury against TCU. Fortunately, the Carolina Panthers still made him a 2nd round pick. Should Texas fans worry about replacing Brooks? Nope. CJ Baxter played gamely for a banged up true freshman in complement to Brooks and he still has upside potential, but the real late season revelation was unlocking Jaydon Blue's explosive speed and quickness.

Blue and Baxter should be an effective duo, but ball security will be key. Despite great early success running and receiving against the Washington Huskies in the playoff game, both Baxter and Blue had crippling 3rd quarter fumbles which effectively prevented Steve Sarkisian from putting the game on their shoulders and exploiting the Huskies' defensive scheme. They will grow from that, but if either falters or falls to injury Texas coaches won't be shy about spinning the wheels on Tre Wisner or the two freshmen.

It's worth noting that Sark threw to the running backs last year more than any time in his history with Brooks, Baxter, Blue and Keilan Robinson combining for 71 catches. Some of that was on checkdowns, but Sark also embraced a creative screen game that's unlikely to go away given that every back on the roster is at least a plus receiver. Additionally, Quinn Ewers exhibits high proficiency in throwing behind the line of scrimmage to his backs. Texas will not be shy about flexing out Blue and Wisner to hunt linebackers and slower safeties. Expect the running backs to be heavily targeted again in 2024, particularly as a dangerous pack of wide outs force opposing defensive coordinators to make some costly concessions underneath.

WIDE RECEIVER

Player	Height	Weight	Class
Isaiah Bond	5'11"	180	JR
Silas Bolden	5'8"	160	SR
DeAndre Moore Jr.	6'0"	195	SO
Johntay Cook	6'0"	185	SO
Matthew Golden	6'0"	195	JR
Ryan Wingo	6'2"	210	FR
Parker Livingstone	6'4"	195	FR
Aaron Butler	6'0"	175	FR
Ryan Niblett	5'10"	185	FR/RS
Thatcher Milton	5'10"	185	SR
Freddie Dubose	6'1"	185	FR

Call him Bond. **Isaiah Bond.** Naturally, Bond wears #007 for the Longhorns and Texas faithful hope he'll be as deadly to Sooners, Bulldogs and Aggies as his namesake is to evil billionaires with space lasers who like to monologue their diabolical plans and then set their devastating weapons on a timer. The football Bond likes beating timers as well. The speedy former Alabama receiver decided that if you can't beat 'em, join 'em and the junior from Buford, GA has the potential to beat a lot of cornerbacks who won't be able to join him when he decides to engage his jets on a go route. Last year, Bond totaled 48 catches for 668 yards and while efficiency metrics didn't love him, attribute that to the growing pains of Jalen Milroe and Bama offensive coordinator Tommy Rees rather than Bond. Bond transferred to

Texas to play with a more complete passer and a strong offensive architect who won't keep his license to thrill under deep cover.

Bond's strength is pure acceleration and separation. He's the human embodiment of "If he's even, he's leaving" and his ability to threaten defenses on verticals will open up the field for the entire offense. If Bond has a weakness, it's that he can suffer occasional drops from anticipating his next move after the catch rather than securing the rock and though he is reasonably nifty side-to-side, he's more comfortable on the run as a vertical athlete. Bama fans still resent his departure, but they can solace themselves with the fact that Bond was the pass catcher that gave them the now legendary 4th and 31 "Grave Digger" touchdown against Auburn that preserved the Tide's playoff bid and humiliated their fiercest rival in Jordan-Hare. Bond lives on forever in Iron Bowl lore. Time to write his name in legend in the Cotton Bowl.

Matthew Golden is another talented transfer wideout with game-changing explosiveness. It doesn't take many film frames to see that he generates raw horsepower like a Ford Mustang peeling out in a high school parking lot and that he is as tough to corral once he gets moving. A highly regarded 4 star receiver from Klein Cain, Golden stayed in his hometown of Houston (when the Horns were too late in offering) and became arguably the most decorated receiver recruit in decades. Golden was a major weapon for the Cougars when healthy – he scored 7 touchdowns as a true freshman – but the health caveat is key. Golden's penchant for nagging soft tissue injuries over the last two years is a concern. However, when he can go, defenses feel his presence. A healthy Golden tortured Texas last year with 7 catches for 88 yards and 2 touchdowns, but groin and turf toe injuries made him an inconsistent performer or a game day scratch for much of the rest of the season. Golden still managed to tally 8 total touchdowns as a sophomore despite limited snaps including a pair of remarkable kickoff return touchdowns on only nine total returns.

Golden is a strong, muscled up athlete who accelerates through arm tackles and his stop-start can be extremely deceptive. He's terrific after the catch once he gets going. Texas knows Golden's explosive potential and an offseason emphasis on injury mitigation could unlock a big contract year. Given Longhorn depth at the position and Golden's history of injury, placing him on a pitch count is probably a good idea. Golden adds massive potential impact as a kick returner.

Silas Bolden arrived in Austin in early summer and the early reports of out of player led drills and 7 on 7 are positive. While the northwestern mighty mite physically profiles as a pure slot, he's surprisingly capable of playing outside. In fact, the Beavers played him only 101 snaps in the slot and 460 outside last year. He also lined up some in the backfield and his skill set certainly begs for gadget plays and trickeration.

What the Texas coaches are certain of is that Bolden is a cat quick playmaker who plays with a massive chip on his shoulder. The diminutive Corvallis standout – whose enviable nickname is The Beaver Joystick – caught 54 balls for 746 yards and five scores last year and over the course of his career he's been an exceptional reverse and jet sweep runner averaging nearly 10 yards per carry with four career rushing touchdowns. Against Utah, the Utes stacked the box against the Beaver running game and Bolden accounted for 153 yards from scrimmage on 8 touches with two touchdowns, earning Game MVP honors in a 21-7 win. He's fully capable of taking over games against defenses that struggle with quickness, but he's most deadly as a high leverage playmaker rather than an every down mainstay.

Bolden is also a capable returner (he brought back a punt against UC-Davis last year), but he's not at Matthew Golden's level. Silas is a veteran 5th year player who played for a hard-nosed Oregon State program and at the very minimum, he'll provide a terrific change up to Texas' array of more conventional fastball receivers. Don't be surprised when you see Bolden high pointing downfield or winning jump balls – he plays much bigger than his diminutive size.

DeAndre Moore came to Texas from California profiled as a mentally tough and nuanced route runner with good hands, but with average physical gifts vis a vis his four star rated peers. Moore didn't quite live up to that billing. It was an undersell. The S&C fast responder is considered one of the fastest and most explosive athletes on the team and he demonstrated that in a strong Spring game performance. Moore has filled out to just under 200 pounds and coaches rave about his physicality as a blocker and a selfless athlete who will eat a hard hit from a linebacker in order to move the sticks underneath. He will contest the incoming transfers for a starting or co-equal role and he has a bright future at Texas.

Johntay Cook is already demonstrating high level ball skills and route running and last year he showed real flashes as a true freshman with 8 catches for 136 yards in spot action. He is quicker than he is straight line fast, but that's because his quickness is elite. Like his classmate DeAndre Moore, Cook won't simply accept the suggested hierarchy of the transfer receivers and he will fight to stake his claim for a starting role or co-equal playing time. Cook's quickness and route running is well understood, but in practices and in the Spring Game, he repeatedly demonstrated elite hands. While Cook may not have Golden or Bond's outright explosiveness, his quickness, hands and route-running intangibles make him an inviting target.

Ryan Wingo is a true freshman in a talented group of receivers, but the coveted recruit from Missouri has a set of traits that make him unique in any locker room in the country. The 6-2, 210 pound Wingo was sold as a physical phenom who would have to learn the finer points of the position, but a Spring Game debut that featured 4 catches for 81 yards and 2 touchdowns revealed that his athletic reputation was well-earned, but it's paired with a much more advanced set of soft skills than anticipated and an ease of movement usually seen in athletes 30 pounds lighter. Wingo will force his way on the field somehow – it's hard to keep talent that precocious under wraps – but August and September practices will tell us how often and in what role. Steve Sarkisian raves about Wingo's work ethic and attitude, suggesting that the coaches may push him a bit in August to see exactly what he can handle with respect to the playbook.

Ryan Niblett is a redshirt freshman whose game is less refined than his 2023 class peers Cook and Moore, but Niblett offers pure RPMs and elite football speed. He ran a 10.4 100 meters and 21.25 200 meters as a high school junior and every bit of that translates to the gridiron. The raw athlete has a running back frame and his yards-after-catch ability is intriguing, but he will need some refinement and reps to fully blossom. Niblett probably won't play a significant role until the log jam ahead of him clears up, but he has real potential to contribute in 2025 and beyond if he can eschew the inevitable portal courting that will come his way.

Parker Livingstone, **Aaron Butler** and **Freddie Dubose** are true freshmen who flew a bit under the radar compared to their class compatriot Wingo, but early reports are all solid. They will have little opportunity to contribute this year, but that's a function of the quality ahead of them.

Thatcher Milton is a high quality walk-on who had a terrific spring capped off by a strong final scrimmage. Thatcher ran through freshmen Texas defensive backs like they were Argentines in the Falklands and though he's unlikely to log many snaps, it's impressive that the Horns can field walk-ons of his quality both on and off of the field. Milton is a former finalist for the Houston Touchdown Club Defensive Player of The Year and a mechanical engineering major. Psst. . .someone might want to hire this guy.

Prognosis

Texas lost a pair of elite wide receivers in Xavier Worthy and Adonai Mitchell. They were production monsters and one of the most dangerous combos in the nation, combining for 130 catches, 1859 yards and 16 touchdowns. Worthy went in the 1st round of the NFL draft (after setting the all-time combine 40 record with a 4.21) and Mitchell didn't last too much longer than that, going with the 52nd pick in the 2nd round.

Texas won't start any two receivers as good as that combo in 2024. The offense also lost veteran team leader Jordan Whittington, who contributed 42 catches and 505 yards. In all, those three receivers combined for a hefty 260 targets. To illustrate the gap between #3 and #4, Johntay Cook had a meager 12 targets. Sark didn't just put all of his eggs in one basket, he put the chickens in there too. Throw in departed tight end JT Sanders' 67 targets and Texas sees 327 of its 445 (73.5%) 2023 season targets evaporate. That should be incredibly disconcerting when projecting the 2024 passing attack. Is Texas headed for a major drop-off?

No, probably not. The transfer portal and the maturation of young talent short circuit conventional analysis (returning production, starters, targets) that has long been reliable and now forces analysts into different calculations.

It's strange to suggest that the receiver two deep got stronger with the departure of Texas' three best receivers, but that is probably the case. The offense now boasts six potentially high level wide receivers of varying skill sets and ability. While the 2023 Horns indisputably had a stronger 1-2 punch, they can't compete with 2024 on receivers 3-6 and overall depth. That raises an interesting question for Steve Sarkisian and wide receiver coach Chris Jackson – how does everyone eat? Sark has long preferred to find his three ride-or-die pass catchers and ride them all year. The reasons are straightforward: familiarity fosters better execution, a short bench racks up chemistry-inducing game reps and it keeps pass catchers on the same page with their quarterback. It also allows Sark to easily introduce more complexity, if or when needed.

Yet the sheer depth and quality of the Longhorn depth chart may force a different approach. Texas has many mouths to feed and it may not be wise to turn half of them away from the passing game soup kitchen. Texas could attack opposing defensive backfields relentlessly with quality numbers – a short rotation of wide outs will inevitably take plays off and pick their spots – but an endless wave of good players wearing on opposing cornerbacks can leg out every backside decoy deep route and attack every run block. Fresh legs can dominate both the 4th quarter and the back half of a season that Longhorn faithful hope lasts until late January.

Sark won't sacrifice effective execution for participatory playing time, but it's difficult to imagine sidelining high level receiving talent that would start for 80% of FBS teams in a playoff era that could ask the Horns to play as many as 15 or 16 games. From a player personnel and roster management perspective, the staff must also factor in an open portal era where all three incoming transfers view this year as one and done. Is it worth discouraging successors Moore, Cook and Wingo?

This is a good problem to have and there is no easy answer. Texas will boast a top ten national unit no matter how one slices it, but whether there is a more diffuse distribution of targets and snaps remains to be seen. This preview's best guess is that Sark uses playbook knowledge, reliability, effort and consistency as the differentiator for starting jobs while still engaging the non-starters with real and meaningful snaps.

TIGHT END

Player	Height	Weight	Class
Gunnar Helm	6'5"	250	SR
Amari Niblack	6'4"	245	SR
Spencer Shannon	6'7"	255	FR/RS
Jordan Washington	6'4"	250	FR
Will Randle	6'4"	240	FR/RS

Gunnar Helm takes center stage as the most experienced tight end on the roster. He logged 493 snaps last year despite being tight end #2. If you view indispensability on the roster as to whether any other player can provide what another starter does in totality in terms of experience and versatility, Helm is pretty darn indispensable. The big Coloradan from Cherry Creek has improved every year at Texas and the 4th year senior has already accumulated ten starts and 39 appearances in his Longhorn career. Helm possesses good feet for a 6-5, 250+ pound athlete and he has always had underrated hands, despite only 19 career catches. That modest number is a reflection of the high level skill players around him rather than Helm's inadequacy as a pass catcher. Expect Helm to see a career high number of targets and receptions this year. Helm and the Longhorn offense would benefit immensely if he can improve both as an in-line blocker and motion fullback from the backfield. Texas needs blockers who can win at the point of attack, not just occupy or aim for a tie.

Amari Niblack comes to Texas from Alabama and the fleet tight end will be an interesting complement to Gunnar Helm and the other Longhorn pass catchers. The rangy Floridian presents a big target who can absolutely fly, as evidenced by his 39 yard touchdown catch against Texas in Tuscaloosa. Niblack totaled 20 catches for 327 yards and 4 touchdowns in 358 snaps over 14 games for Bama, forfeiting snaps against certain matchups when the Tide had to bring on bigger tight ends to help their leaky pass protection. There is a general impression amongst some Longhorn faithful and media that Niblack will be TE #1 due to his recruiting pedigree and pass catching skill set, but that may be a fundamental misunderstanding of the tight end's role in Sark's offense and the balance and playbook mastery that he demands from the position. Helm is currently the lead tight end and Amari would need to show new dimensions to his game to displace him. Niblack's pure speed is undeniable though – his first five or ten yards from his stance are indistinguishable from a wide receiver – and he has a dangerous role to play for Texas when Longhorn receivers draw inordinate coverage attention.

Juan Davis has Juan in a million athleticism, but hasn't been able to employ it much yet on the field. At one point during the offseason, Davis entered the portal, but portaled back to Texas. Portaling across time/space only to return to his starting point may have military applications, so it's possible that he returned for Lockheed NIL money. Juan has long needed to gain weight and spend more time in the playbook, but some positive Sarkisian comments from this spring suggest that he may be doing just that.

Spencer Shannon is a skyscraper tight end who is still growing into his body. He is currently viewed more as a blocker, but he will need to fill out his 6-7 frame for his full realization as such.

Will Randle was Arch Manning's #1 target in high school and the flypaper handed tight end will need more time to build his body up for the college game.

Jordan Washington is a true freshman who impressed considerably in the spring and has already added 35+ pounds to his long, athletic frame. He has 10.5 inch hands and the former basketball standout has already exhibited the ability to win jump balls in the seam. Keep an eye on Mr Washington. His future is bright.

Prognosis

Despite a deep receiving room, Texas won't be shy about continuing to employ two tight end sets to hunt for certain coverages or attack defenses in the running game that choose to go with light personnel. Over the last two years, Texas has spent a surprising number of snaps with two tight ends on the field, ranking them in the Top 10 in college football in that personnel grouping. While Texas would have certainly welcomed JT Sanders' return for another year and no other individual tight end will match his 67 target, 45 catch, 682 yard 2023 production, the Horns should be able to do enough of what they want with a healthy Gunnar Helm and the situational possibilities of the fleet-footed Amari Niblack to get by adequately. Expect more of the passing game to be diverted to the talented running backs and wide outs.

OFFENSIVE LINE

Player	Height	Weight	Class
Kelvin Banks	6'4"	320	JR
Cameron Williams	6'5"	335	JR
Daniel Cruz	6'3"	310	FR
DJ Campbell	6'3"	330	JR
Cole Hutson	6'5"	310	JR
Connor Robertson	6'4"	310	SO
Jake Majors	6'3"	315	SR
Malik Agbo	6'4"	300	SO
Max Merrill	6'4"	295	JR
Nate Kibble	6'3"	320	FR
Neto Umeozulu	6'4"	330	SO
Brandon Baker	6'4"	315	FR
Trevor Goosby	6'7"	315	FR/RS
Jaydon Chatman	6'4"	300	FR/RS
Hayden Conner	6'5"	320	SR
Andre Cojoe	6'6"	340	FR/RS
Connor Stroh	6'7"	350	FR/RS

Kelvin Banks is currently predicted to be a top half of the 1st round pick in the 2025 NFL draft so this is likely the junior left tackle's last season in Austin. With 27 starts over his career and 1,840 game snaps logged, the 2023 1st team All Big 12 selection and 2nd team All-American has been a steady rock and a dominant pass protector during his time in Austin. He allows pressure on only 2.2% of dropbacks. Despite his relative youth, he's a game-tested veteran. Banks was a revelation in his freshman season, starting all 13 games for the Longhorns at left tackle. Aside from the rarity of college freshmen being useful starters anywhere, much less the offensive line, starting one at left tackle is nearly suicidal. Banks turned in the most impressive true freshman offensive tackle performance in Longhorn history, earning 2nd team All-Big 12 honors from the coaches and freshman All-American accolades from multiple outlets. Those plaudits undersell the quality of his play. He acquitted himself well against Alabama's Will Anderson and Texas Tech's Tyree Wilson, more than held his own against Iowa State's Will McDonald and won his matchup against Kansas State's Felix Anudike-Uzomah. All four edge players were 1st round NFL draft picks.

Two years later, he's still getting better. Banks possesses excellent feet and good technique, but his competitive determination is unmatched. Kelvin rarely makes mental errors and his effort is unrelenting. Banks was an elite pass protector in 2022 and he exceeded that performance as a sophomore. Banks finished in the top 10 of all college pass blockers and after Week 8, he was the highest graded pass blocking offensive tackle in college football per Pro Football Focus. Banks is a willing run blocker with the agility and footwork to dominate smaller defenders, but he occasionally struggles to get displacement on bigger linemen at the point of attack. He's more technician than road grader against 300+ pounders, but 2023 featured several instances of Banks blowing up 2nd and 3rd level defenders downfield on screens and run plays. His run blocking should improve in Year 3 and his outstanding pass blocking acumen is not a perishable skill. Texas fans should appreciate such a high effort, high character talent in his final year in Austin.

Fifth year senior center **Jake Majors** has notched a team-leading 41 starts with over 2700 snaps registered in his career at Texas. The three time Academic 1st Team All-Big 12 selection took a major(s) leap forward in his overall play last year vs. his first three years of action despite playing the back half of the year with a debilitating high ankle sprain sustained on the 1st drive of the game against Oklahoma.

That ankle sprain knocked him out of the game in Dallas, but he didn't miss another start for the rest of the year despite the initial diagnosis that he would be out for 6-8 weeks. Majors cowboyed up and played through a lot of pain, earning the respect of teammates and coaches. Majors also capped the year with his best performance of the season against Washington in the playoffs. This was likely not coincidental to the fact that he was finally able to heal up his ankle rather than re-injuring it every week. Given his overall improvement last year despite injury after three previous years that suggested a performance plateau, it's not improbable that Texas will see another bump in play from Majors in 2024. That flies against the perception that he has maxed out his ceiling in Austin, but five years of college football can allow a body to improve even as the mind slows the game down.

Majors has not been particularly powerful at the point of contact in the running game, but he has active feet, does a great job of getting his hands on opposing defenders with inside leverage and he is good at coordinating line calls. Only a handful of college centers are as experienced and it's remarkable to think that Majors will have started as many as 55 games by the time his career in Austin concludes. Majors has likely seen every stunt and front known to man and that should prove very useful, particularly in an early season matchup in Ann Arbor against a talented, blitz heavy defense. Majors is also agile enough to act as a puller from the center position, which Texas has had him do to good effect against certain fronts. Historically, Majors has struggled to hold up against powerful nose tackles, but that problem cleared up a bit last year, at least as a pass protector. Majors may be a borderline NFL draft prospect, but the vast majority of college offensive coordinators would crawl over broken glass for a player as experienced, tough and smart.

Hayden Conner is a 4th year senior with 27 consecutive career starts spanning the last two seasons. The massive guard fits Kyle Flood's preferred size requirements for Big Humans which is another way of saying that he fits the size requirements for the protagonist in a Godzilla movie. Conner is a top 10% pass protector on the interior offensive line. He's smart, plays with awareness and has addressed an early career bad habit of lunging at defenders. He keeps a good base in pass protection and has realized that if he keeps a strong posture, light feet and heavy hands, there aren't many college defensive tackles who can bull rush his 320 pound frame.

Conner must level up as a run blocker, where he has been, at best, a middling performer. He tries to screen rather than drive defenders and he isn't "sticky" enough at contact – meaning defenders slide him off of him too easily after initial contact and then pursue the ball. Raw power is largely an innate quality and #76 may not have a natural abundance to help him with his initial shock and drive off of the snap that enable displacement, but pad level, strength and technique enable stickiness to be improved and refined for any guard. If Conner levels up a run blocker, the Texas run game will prosper, particularly in the red zone and in short yardage. It is worth noting that Conner can capably play center and right tackle as well, so it is possible that he could be called on in a pinch at either spot.

Cameron Williams is noticeably gigantic on an offensive line of giants. The junior tackle from Duncanville is absolutely massive but also has surprising athleticism for his size. He is currently expected to hold down starting right tackle, but some growing pains should be anticipated given his lack of experience, particularly as a pass blocker. Interestingly, Williams started 76 snaps last year against Kansas State and more than held his own in pass protection, but struggled at times to adjust on run assignments against a shifting front. Later, he earned 24 snaps in the blowout win over Texas Tech and he showed flashes of brilliance as a run blocker. When a defensive player simply lines up in front of him and plays a base technique, that defender is in for an extended grizzly bear mauling that makes what happened to Hugh Glass in The Revenant look like child's play. Williams will likely struggle more with slants and pre-snap movement than space-eaters and big bodies.

The NFL talent is there, the question is how quickly it emerges. Williams has seen spot action, but he will be the clear experiential outlier on the seasoned 2024 offensive line. Williams has reshaped his body, but he has a bit more to go to eliminate some stiffness and reach his full potential. This summer and Fall camp will be particularly important for him. Watching #56 on film can be a treat. Williams has heavy hands and it's amusing to watch 250+ pound defenders rag doll away from him violently when it looks like Big Cam did nothing more than offer routine contact or a lazy paw across their chest. His progress at right tackle will set the ceiling for the 2024 Texas offensive line.

DJ Campbell has played in 21 games, including 14 starts last year as a 2nd year sophomore. The former 5 star recruit did not have the luxury of a redshirt so now the 3rd year junior is still addressing an understandable learning curve. Campbell might be the most naturally powerful offensive lineman on the team – with Cam Williams in strong contention – but he needs to make technical improvement as a pass protector, better understand line calls against moving fronts and exhibit better general awareness. He understandably struggled early last year making rookie starts on a veteran offensive line, but it is a cardinal sin for interior offensive linemen to give free runs to the quarterback by botching line calls. Campbell did this too often in the first half of the season. Campbell did have some standout games (Alabama, Iowa State, Texas Tech) but finished the year with a middling grade overall due to rough outings in other contests. Campbell still has ample opportunity to level up across the board and when assignment certainty catches up with his physical traits, he could be excellent. The coaches have several strong options on the interior that will push him for starting snaps.

One thing to consider for Campbell is that he and Cam Williams are the least experienced members of the unit, but are the most explosive run blockers mano-a-mano and are capable of getting real push at the point of attack. This is a valuable trait for one side of the line to have, offering the potential for key 3rd and short conversions and better red zone rushing success than what Texas saw last year.

Cole Hutson was the sole early enrollee for the much hyped 2022 offensive line class and less heralded than most of his peers, but he still earned a starting job at right guard as a true freshman. That is a positive reflection on Hutson's maturity and competitiveness but a negative reflection of the offensive line recruiting and development under the prior regime. If Hutson was supposed to be the high floor program guy that the coaches brought along slowly, the physical young guard did not get the memo. Hutson started 13 games as a true freshman and while he had some struggles (he allowed 24 pressures, a team high), he proved himself a gutty and game competitor willing to play through injury. Immediately after the season, Hutson had surgery on a torn labrum that prevented him from going through spring practice and offseason S&C development.

In 2023, in part because of his inability to participate in offseason development and also due to sitting out the opener against Rice with a practice injury, DJ Campbell closed ground on Hutson in the battle for starting right guard, securing co-starter status. They split time when Hutson returned the following week (Cole logged 43 snaps against Alabama) but a knee injury against Wyoming sidelined Hutson for several weeks and gave Campbell the needed daylight to wrap up the starter's role for the rest of the year. Cole logged another 100 or so snaps in spot action when he returned, but constant injuries have sabotaged his development and opportunity. From a developmental perspective, the 3rd year junior guard badly needs an entire offseason of full S&C participation to get stronger, reshape his body and gain more technical skills as a pass blocker. If he can do that, expect him to push Campbell in August and, at minimum, provide excellent depth on the Longhorn interior both at guard and center (the latter could be his best future projection in 2025).

Neto Umeozulu is a 3rd year sophomore from Allen and one of the most talented offensive linemen on the team. He's big, default aggressive and moves very well for his size. The staff likes his long term trajectory. The main issue preventing more playing time is a lack of game reps, the 54 games of cumulative starting experience split over the three guards ahead of him and a tendency towards careless mental errors that makes it difficult to jump him over a known quantity. Other programs know what Umeozulu has to offer and some have been in contact, but the interior depth chart clears up considerably in 2025 and thus far Neto has been content to wait and play the long game for his junior and senior seasons.

Trevor Goosby is a skyscraper offensive tackle still learning his craft, but the Longhorn coaches love his development and competitiveness. They would prefer to unveil him to opponents in 2025 rather than 2024 as the big man would benefit from more weight and strength to solidify his base. The former discus and shot competitor has good coordination and feet and takes football seriously.

Malik Agbo is a 3rd year sophomore that played snaps last year as a jumbo package tight end in short yardage situations. That earned him 122 snaps of game action and a six yard catch against Washington in the playoffs. Agbo projects to tackle, but he needs to gain weight and strength to make a push in 2024 and beyond.

Connor Robertson is a third year center from Austin Westlake who garnered 124 snaps last year, including 75 snaps against the Oklahoma Sooners when Jake Majors went down on the 4th play of the game. The inexperienced Robertson was forced into a chaotic environment against a Venables defense that pulled out every stop to confuse the young center. Though he struggled, Robertson gave his best in an unthinkably difficult situation. He will battle Cole Hutson for the backup center role in 2024 and then both Hutson and Daniel Cruz for the starting gig in 2025.

Jayden Chatman is a redshirt freshman who has added good size since coming to Texas as an underweight but physical guard. He adds depth in a crowded guard room, but has the feet to play tackle in a pinch.

Andre Cojoe turned 17 years old just a few days after enrolling at Texas. Given his age and massive frame, it's a good bet that the second year freshman will play his best football in Austin in his 4th and 5th years as his young body gets more coordinated, trimmed up and powerful. Cojoe's development will happen in a crockpot, not the microwave. Put on a lid, hit S&C simmer and check back in a few.

Connor Stroh is one of the strongest players in the program, but his future efficacy will be determined by his ability to manage his weight, master his footwork, develop technical skill and stay patient. Like his classmate Cojoe, Stroh will have a longer trajectory of development. Future guard. If it comes together, Texas could have a monster inside. If it doesn't, there's a reason that Flood takes big OL classes every year.

Max Merril is a 4th year junior who will add depth.

Brandon Baker, **Daniel Cruz** and **Nate Kibble** form a strong 2024 offensive line class. Many consider Cruz one of the best natural center prospects in the state of Texas over the last decade, Kibble is a cold-blooded run game mauler from Atascocita and Baker was a highly sought after blue chip from California powerhouse Mater Dei. All of them should be able to redshirt, but Flood is never shy about throwing a precocious standout into the two deep if their August camp impresses.

Prognosis

The Texas offensive line brings back five players with a combined 122 starts. That becomes six players with 123 combined starts when you add right tackle Cam Williams. Williams is the only inexperienced likely starter and there's a good chance that his ability to maul defenders will overcome his experiential gaffes if Texas fans are sufficiently patient. Overall unit starting experience and returning production ranks in the top 15% of college football. Few offensive lines can match the battle tested nature of the Majors-Conner-Banks troika with the Longhorn center and left side combo notching a combined 95 starts and more than 6,000 college game reps between them. Pass protection should be an overall unit strength and run blocking could improve if the right side can bring the hate as expected and if Majors, Conner and Banks can all show improvement to their baseline.

Guard has the greatest depth of starting experience with three players (Conner-Campbell-Hutson) accounting for 54 combined starts (27-14-13). Then consider that the most physically talented backup on the entire line might be the 4th guard Neto Umeozulu. Guard has a great depth floor. Now it's time for players like Conner and Campbell/Hutson to stretch the ceiling. Conner has to block the run better, Hutson needs to stay healthy and Campbell can't miss assignments.

The Longhorn staff has done a fine job restocking the cupboard on the recruiting trail and comparing the two and three deep in 2024 to when Steve Sarkisian first arrived in Austin is encouraging, if not rage-inducing. Continuity in coaching with offensive line coach Kyle Flood has meant continuity in philosophy: Texas wants big humans, period. Any recruit that doesn't fit that profile is likely exceptional in several other key areas and they won't be small either.

The Big Humans methodology doesn't just mean coveting size, it also means gathering Many Big Humans. It means throwing numbers at the offensive line at the expense of additional wide receivers or running backs. Sark has agreed to the necessary precondition of the big human philosophy panning optimally – get a lot of 'em and let teaching and S&C cull the herd. Offensive linemen are hard to project and the staff understands that a lot of bites at the apple (with an accompanying vitality curve to trapdoor non-developers) is the more humble and practical approach to success rather than believing that they can pick and choose winners with surgical precision. Prior regimes believed they could and they were inevitably wrong.

Given the option of which offensive line positions to load up on experience, pick center and left tackle. Texas boasts 68 starts between the two. Experience isn't limited to those two spots either. Eight different returning Longhorn offensive linemen logged 100+ snaps in 2023 (including Malik Agbo's snaps at jumbo tight end).

Decision maker starts are important. Who are the primary on-field decision makers on offense who direct other players on what to do? The center and quarterback. Overall unit and offensive cohesion should be outstanding with Jake Majors and Quinn Ewers boasting a combined 63 college starts (22 of those starts playing together) in their 3rd shared year running Steve Sarkisian's offense. This is not a trivial observation. Combined decision maker starts suggests an advanced ability to get out of a bad play or line call to something better with the confidence that only comes with experience. Inexperience at center or QB can short circuit the advantage of having experience at the other. Combined experience from both allows timely, accurate and lower stress pre-snap adjustments. Calm is contagious. The ability to adjust on the fly over a time span of plays, drives, or at most a quarter, is markedly different from having to wait until halftime...or the postgame Sunday film session after a loss because the defense threw out a wrinkle that couldn't be solved in real time.

If the Texas offense is going to maximize and create early leads that will enable the Longhorn defense to unleash what should be a much improved pass rush, the play of the offensive line is paramount. Texas has the talent and experience to field a very good unit. Now it's time to do it.

DEFENSIVE TACKLE

Player	Height	Weight	Class
Bill Norton	6'6"	335	SR
Vernon Broughton	6'4"	305	SR
Aaron Bryant	6'2"	305	SO
Melvin Hills	6'3"	305	FR
Jaray Bledsoe	6'4"	290	SO
Sydir Mitchell	6'6"	350	FR/RS
Alfred Collins	6'5"	320	SR
Alex January	6'5"	315	FR
Tiaoalii Savea	6'4"	295	SR
Jermayne Lole	6'3"	315	SR

Alfred Collins must play like a legitimate NFL draft pick if Texas wants to meet their goal of being a major playoff and national title contender. Before last season, Collins focused on gaining weight, committing fully to the notion that he is an inside player. #95 now rolls around at 6-5, 315 without a hint of sloppiness and has the requisite size and strength to handle double teams. He parlayed his new body into a 22 tackle, 2 sack and 5 QB hit season backing up the exceptional combo of Murphy and Sweat while also playing well as a 5 technique edge in jumbo packages. Collins was ranked 2nd in pressure rate (over 11%) among Big 12 defensive linemen and his combination of length and agility at his size means that he can collapse pockets quickly. Alfred's play strength has improved and he is the best pure talent in the interior Longhorn defensive line, but in his 5th and final season in Austin, he needs to find consistent game impact. Texas needs him to become a problem and he needs to play with the every snap intensity of a man in a contract year. The disruptor that the opposing offensive coordinator circles on film and says,"So what's the plan for Collins, gentlemen?" The Horns certainly saw the light turn on for both Sweat and Murphy (if you confidently predicted Murphy as a 1st round draft pick at this time last year and you're not his Mom or Murphy himself, you're a liar), so it's not overly optimistic to imagine a similar final year ceiling for Collins. The tools are certainly there.

Collins is generally at his best as a disruptive 3 technique (outside shoulder of the guard) attacking gaps rather than catching blocks and double teams. That hasn't always jibed with Pete Kwiatkowski's preferences – he loves his defensive tackles to dominate space rather than play through gaps – but stylistically PK probably needs to meet Collins (and the rest of this defensive tackle room) somewhere in the middle. A former basketball standout, Collins has unusual coordination and movement for an athlete of his size and he's doing a better job of maintaining low pads, shedding blocks, getting good hand placement and understanding how blockers are attacking him. Collins' ability to penetrate paired with his wingspan makes him a problem for quick RPO passing games and pairing him with Ethan Burke on the same side presents an imposing wall of hands and arms. For shorter signal callers with a shallow set up trying to throw a quick RPO read, it must feel like trying to throw a volleyball over a redwood. Quinn Ewers learned that in the Spring game with a Burke batted ball interception that enabled a Collins pick-six, which is exactly the kind of big play impact the Horns will need from big Alfred this year.

Vernon Broughton chipped in with 17 tackles and 4.5 tackles for loss backing up Murphy and Sweat. His best season as a Longhorn. As with Collins, Texas needs more from him in his 5th and final season. Broughton skipped the Spring game in order to get married and while the game probably didn't mean much to his overall development, given his tenure, it also didn't scream buy-in and self-awareness. Consequently, Texas brought in two more portal defensive tackles to join the one already on campus. Due to the wedding gaffe, Broughton will have to take his wife's maiden name or be referred to as Mrs. Vernon Broughton for the remainder of 2024. If that infuriates Vernon and forces him into a 7 sack and 15 tackles for loss final season, all the better.

Broughton brings initial explosiveness out of his stance and is capable of a good initial strike on blockers, particularly as a pass rusher, but high pads and an inability to keep leverage prevent him from having a more consistent impact on the field. Last year was the first season in which double teams didn't wash him out completely and he's learning how to better anchor and create a car crash inside when teams run right at him. That isn't always easy for a player that's split high (long legs, short torso) with a naturally lofty center of gravity. For Texas to maximize inside, Broughton needs to progress from above average as a pass rusher to being an actual problem while continuing to improve as a passable run defender with enough athleticism to knife through a gap when PK allows it.

Bill Norton comes to Texas from Arizona, one of three portal interior defensive linemen meant to shore up Longhorn losses inside. The gigantic Tennessee native began his college career at Georgia, where he was a fairly touted recruit, but he transferred to Tucson and didn't earn a starting job until last year. He joins the Longhorns for his 6th and final year of college football. Norton is a solid player who played his best ball down the backstretch of last season. Last year was by far the best ball of his entire career. He is a negligible pass rusher in terms of sacks – he's not going to chase down the passer and finish the play – but he is active getting hurries, pushing the pocket and batting down balls. His best asset is that he fills up the box score with subtle plays and helps create for others. Norton will likely play over the center as a nose tackle and though Texas fans won't confuse his range or striking power with Poona Ford or Casey Hampton, he's a big 'ol boy that's reasonably active, runs line games credibly and is not just a block magnet looking to cause pile-ups. Norton was brought in to combat some of the high level running games that Texas is guaranteed to face and serve as an extra active body in what should be a hockey line shift approach to the interior.

Tiaoalii Savea was Bill Norton's partner-in-crime in Tucson where he was an effective slanting run defender and had little to no impact as a pass rusher. Savea doesn't fit the stereotype of the squatty Polynesian run stopper who can't be moved from his spot. In fact, he's a bit of a finesse, hustle and movement-focused run supporter who excels running line games, slanting, moving laterally and confusing blocking schemes to make plays rather than overwhelming guards with pure play strength. The

Wildcat bowl game against the Sooners was probably Savea's best game of the season and that may have given some Longhorn fans an inflated perception of Savea's potential impact, but the Sooners were without a starting guard and center and they struggled to deal with Arizona's line stunts and movement up front from both a physical and coordination standpoint. Savea was an important get for depth and rotation purposes and it will be interesting to see how and if Texas varies its approach up front to take advantage of Savea's movement-oriented skill set.

Jermayne Lole flipped to Texas from Oklahoma in early May, the Longhorns' third and final interior portal piece. He could have a wide range of potential impact. As wide as third team on the depth chart to forcing his way into the starting line-up. What Lole brings up front is a mystery given a star-crossed career that saw injuries diminish a once terrific player. Lole began his career at Arizona State and racked up 123 tackles, 20 tackles for loss and 11 sacks in just under two and a half years and in 2019 he notched an outstanding 38 pressures on the quarterback. Coming into 2021, Pro Football Focus rated him as a Top 10 defensive tackle nationally. Then it all fell apart. He missed the entire 2021 season with injuries and played in only two games in 2022 after transferring to Louisville. After recovering from that season ending elbow injury, he was able to notch a complete season in 2023 playing 411 snaps for a solid Cardinal defense. He appeared in 12 games, starting 9. His play was clearly diminished from 2019-2020 levels, but he was a reasonable cog in the defense. Last year, Lole didn't show much of the burst that had once made him a terrifying interior pass rusher and overall disruptor and whether that's recoverable in his 7th season of eligibility seems improbable. At minimum, he's a super experienced player who can be a part of the rotation inside. No idea what Lole has left in the tank as he has not played at a really high level since 2020. August camp will quickly tell the tale.

Jaray Bledsoe is a third year sophomore with serious raw ability who has finally added the necessary weight to be an interior player. He missed his senior year of high school due to an eligibility issue and you certainly can't blame him for a lack of historical playing time given the presence of players like Ojomo, Murphy, Sweat and Collins ahead of him on the depth chart over the last two years. However, it's time for Jaray to step up and shine. Bledsoe flashes in practice, particularly as a penetrator and pass rusher, but he lacks consistency and buy-in on the details that foster trust from the coaches both on and off of the field. Few draw as many raves for upside potential from other players, but until Bledsoe matures and understands that he has to bring it on every down and in every practice rep, he will limit his opportunity and the staff will turn to more mature, even if less talented, options. Bledsoe needs the light to come on soon or risk being recruited over. Texas badly needs his emergence given a paper thin 2025 defensive tackle room.

Sydir Mitchell is every bit of 6-6, 350+ and the redshirt freshman from Paterson, New Jersey inhabits multiple zip codes on the defensive line. Like Bledsoe, he has all of the potential in the world. The issue is his urgency to maximize. Sydir is carrying bad weight and the Spring game was a good example of what makes him both so tantalizing and frustrating. Early in a drive, Texas blockers could do nothing with him. He is too huge and powerful. For a while, at least. By the end of the drive, after experiencing an anaerobic deficit from running around a little, he was getting pancaked into the end zone by Cameron Williams. He's not in football shape and fatigue makes cowards of us all. The good news about being out of shape at his size is that if one can get through an initial three weeks of real discomfort, it doesn't take much to show meaningful improvement and find some wind. Sydir is one productive off season away from putting himself in a position to become a powerful and coveted presence inside. Mitchell will play a long time in the NFL if he decides he wants to make the effort necessary to make it happen. His God-given power and ability to anchor are rare gifts. The question is whether that realization happens at Texas, at his second or third stop, or never at all.

Aaron Bryant is a redshirt sophomore from Mississippi who has seen limited action in his young Longhorn career. He is perceived as having a stable floor rather than a soaring ceiling and the recruitment of Norton, Savea and Lole speak to the staff's current impression of his readiness to play major snaps.

Alex January and **Melvin Hills** are true freshmen. Right now, January has the better opportunity to play early as the early enrollee impressed Longhorn coaches with his effort and maturity. Hills will be a longer term project.

DEFENSIVE EDGE

Player	Height	Weight	Class
Justice Finkley	6'2"	250	JR
Trey Moore	6'3"	245	JR
Collin Simmons	6'3"	245	FR
Barryn Sorrell	6'4"	260	SR
Ethan Burke	6'6"	260	JR
Colton Vasek	6'5"	260	FR/RS
Zina Umeozulu	6'5"	260	FR

Barryn Sorrell is proof that players don't always dramatically break out. Some just get incrementally better every year. He has notched 24 starts with 33 total appearances over his time in Austin and you can safely bet that he'll improve again in his final season at Texas. The 6-4, 260 pound power rushing senior from New Orleans sets the edge well in the run game and does a fine job extending and working through or around blockers. Sorrell is an average to above average pass rusher (4 sacks, 24 hurries, 12 QB hits last year) but typically he's been better at getting pressure than actually finishing the play and he lacks a signature pass rush move.

He also sees a dramatic drop off against high end offensive tackles. Fortunately, there aren't many of those around. His effort level is a given and Sorrell never takes plays off. There is a perception that Sorrell is "maxed out" as a player as he has improved every year in Austin and there are a lot of examples of steady improvement guys fully blossoming or breaking out in their final year. Given the growth of Texas edge talent from last year to this season, Sorrell could actually see fewer snaps (he played 587 last year) but with greater overall game impact.

Ethan Burke is a true junior from Austin Westlake who made a nice leap last year, earning 9 starts and 13 game appearances across from Barryn Sorrell. Burke filled up the box score with 41 tackles, 5.5 sacks, 9 tackles for loss, 19 hurries and 4 QB hits in 434 snaps, but he was situationally replaced by Alfred Collins (and occasionally Vernon Broughton) in jumbo packages when Texas really wanted to destroy an opponent running game.

The 6'6" Burke uses his wingspan well and he should better be able to finish plays as a pass rusher and tackler as he gains more strength. Burke plays the run well on the move when it's going outside of or away from him – he gets excellent separation and doesn't allow blockers to get into his body, allowing him to use his superior agility and wingspan. His ability to anchor and squeeze gaps against off tackle runs aimed right at him should improve over time. The former all-state lacrosse player is very mobile and his combination of length and change of direction makes him a potentially dangerous pass rusher, but he'd benefit from playing a little heavier so that he can add more power to his repertoire. Burke has real breakout potential, but will need to fight for every snap in an elevated edge room.

Colton Vasek was a revelation in the Spring game. The redshirt freshman from Austin Westlake was dominant on the edge, racking up three pressures, a sack (or two – depending on your interpretation of the whistle) and 3.5 tackles for loss. The once slender 6'5" pass rusher has put on good weight (he's up thirty pounds now), mended from nagging injuries and he's bendy, elusive and technical. He uses his hands well, doesn't accept blocking and his motor doesn't quit. Some defenders seem to just magically slip off of blockers after initial contact – they genetically do not accept blocking – and Vasek is one of them. Vasek is a tall guy capable of using all of the advantages of using his height and wingspan, but he can also level change so that he doesn't pay a height tax when he needs to get leverage. That's a rare combo. Texas going from utterly bereft to overrun with quality young edges has been a nice development and it's a good bet that Vasek will force his way on the field, even in a crowded room.

Trey Moore was a major addition in the offseason. Moore was the 2023 AAC Defensive Player of The Year after setting UTSA's single season record for sacks (14) while also adding another 38 pressures and 22 QB hurries. That wasn't a single season anomaly either. In 2022, a redshirt freshman Moore started every game for the Roadrunners and notched 8 sacks, 18 tackles for loss (breaking the all-time UTSA record), 59 tackles, 39 pressures and was named a Freshman All-American. Those are insane disruption numbers and while the level up from lesser competition to the big leagues is never a sure thing, Group of Five studs have a tendency to remain impactful when they move up in competition. Moore will face much better offensive tackles in the SEC, but now he's also surrounded by more gifted teammates who can create opportunities for him.

UTSA liked to free up Trey one-on-one, but Moore was particularly gifted at running down passers flushed by initial pressure from someone else. The 245 pound junior from Smithson Valley is only a mediocre run defender as Moore favors quickness and mobility over brawn, but he excels at pursuit and makes a lot of hustle plays. Though the Roadrunners were smart enough to keep Moore aimed at the quarterback on most passing downs, he is surprisingly competent in coverage and appears capable of dropping into zones or picking up a crosser when needed. He is slated for the rotation at Edge, but he could also easily play the SAM linebacker position that featured Jett Bush last year. In the Longhorn scheme, that position frequently lines up on the line of scrimmage outside and is given free rein to fire into the enemy backfield when not dropping into coverage. That blitz or cover combo feels like a good fit for Moore, but it would require some more imaginative linebacker groupings or fronts to keep Texas from taking the nickel off of the field to allow it. The Horns possess a pure edge pass-rushing asset. Can the Texas defensive scheme maximize him?

Colin Simmons is the bluest of blue chip freshmen and proof that the news on the edge just keeps getting better and better. The five star pass rusher was a legendary disruptor at Duncanville due to a blinding first step and accelerated play speed, but playing Georgia isn't quite like facing Waxahachie, so tap the brakes a bit on predictions of a double digit sack freshman debut. Simmons has already put on good weight and will likely stabilize around 245-255 at some point down the road. Colin is a hard player to keep off of the field, but the wealth of options at edge and his redundancy in skill set to Trey Moore means that the defensive brain trust will need to get creative to employ him fully. Or Texas could preach patience, let him mature into his full powers and unleash him in years to come.

Justice Finkley enters his third year at Texas. This preview was impressed with Finkley's maturity, focus and developed body as a true freshman, but he is a compact 250 pound edge trying to win with motor and strength rather than speed or change of direction. That's a tall order for a short edge and it's simply not scalable, particularly as the locker room adds longer, quicker and more explosive athletes like Moore, Burke, Simmons and Vasek. Finkley can outwork bad or ponderous offensive tackles and he's good on the move when he can attack interior gaps on a stunt, but short edges better have outstanding quickness and power and a killer spin move to make up for their lack of length if they want to be effective pass rushers. So far, that has not been Finkley. There is also a misguided perception that Finkley excels against the run, but that's not really the case. Finkley played 284 snaps last year and that number should decrease absent injuries. He is a capable player with a great work ethic and a good motor who should be called on to provide experienced depth, but unless he can add more suddenness or pass rushing moves to his repertoire, the junior may already be maxed out.

Zina Umeozulu is a raw true freshman with excellent traits that project well down the road. His commitment is clearly another step in getting more length, wingspan and mobility on the edge.

Prognosis

Texas lost the best pair of defensive tackles in the country. No defense can shrug that off, particularly when those defensive tackles were not just individually outstanding but were also employed as a consistent cheat code to enable the rest of the defense. Sweat and Murphy could play any style needed – they could be disruptors or simply dominate and own space playing straight up, demanding at least three and as many as four blockers between the two of them. Their versatility will be missed and it allowed Texas to get away with some things on defense that won't be available anymore. The good news for the 2024 defensive line is that while defensive tackle will take a step back, edge play should take a major step forward.

Will it all even out in the wash? That's possible, even if interior play tends to be a bit more important in structuring an overall defense. In fact, the total defensive line might boast a better three deep than last year, but the Texas defensive brain trust – abetted by new linebacker coach and former Arizona DC Johnny Nansen – needs to reimagine aspects of the front and marry those changes to the second level and the rest of the defense for that to matter. To that end, Texas brought in three solid interior bodies in the portal, which was vital in addressing depth and need, but also a clear indication of what the coaches thought about existing depth and every defensive tackle not named Alfred Collins.

Right now, talented youngsters Jaray Bledsoe and Sydir Mitchell are viewed as unreliable X factors who could emerge, sit or split. If one or both emerges, that would be extremely good news for this season and a couple that follow, but crystal balls are murky and the Texas coaches needed reliability and fewer unknowns. Vernon Broughton played better last year, but is a better change up than a mainstay, Aaron Bryant is viewed as just OK and counting on true freshmen in the SEC is suicide. The staff needed more from the room and they went out and got it by securing two experienced Arizona defensive tackles and Lole.

On balance, the overall trait make-up on the interior now leans more towards movement, slanting, penetration and line games rather than straight up dominance. Whether Pete Kwiatkowski is willing to adjust his approach up front (which could expose new middle linebacker Anthony Hill to more run-fit responsibility) or he simply forces them to develop as run anchors remains to be seen. Either way, Texas now has a reliable core rotation and a valid two deep with the realistic potential of as many as six interior players being game ready and useful. That allows the coaches to attack inside talent loss in the aggregate with a constantly rotating group of defensive tackles that won't tire over the course of a game or season. No single defensive tackle will be asked to exhaust himself and maximal effort should be expended on every down.

Texas also gets to emulate its inner BYU. This is a seasoned defensive tackle group. Lole is a 7th year player, Norton is a 6th, both Broughton and Collins are 5th year players and Savea is a 4th year senior. Maturity should raise the floor and create some stability. At minimum, they should be able to put personnel groups out there that can stand up to bullies – which the Longhorn schedule will not lack, by the way. The realistic goal is to get above average to good defensive tackle play overall. Downgrading from a 9.5 out of 10 at defensive tackle in 2023 to a 7.0 or 7.5 out of 10 in 2024 is a 1st world problem that most programs would envy, but Texas is being graded on a harsh curve. The season goal isn't to win 8 games and go to a bowl game. The goal is a SEC title and a deep playoff run.

What about the edges?

In 2022, Texas led the country in pressures but finished with only 20 sacks in 13 games. Last year, Texas totaled 32 sacks in 14 games. That's not all on the Longhorn edges, but the Horns still need to finish better or get pressure to begin with – that was a glaring problem in losses to Oklahoma and Washington and it nearly cost them a road upset at TCU. Some of that is on the Longhorn secondary needing to challenge receivers more on key downs so the rush can get home, but a good bit of it is also on Texas defensive linemen not finishing plays and an edge room that really struggled even getting started against higher end pass blocking units. They didn't finish quarterbacks that the defensive tackles flushed to them from the pocket enough.

That's about to change. With Burke and Sorrell guaranteed to improve, Santa bringing new pass rush wind up toys in Trey Moore and Colin Simmons, the emergence of the dynamic Colton Vasek and some really exciting young recruits, Texas now has an edge room to envy. Which of them should Texas play? All of them. Well, at least four or five of them. And they should feel empowered to play like maniacs, knowing that they don't have to go 65 snaps, but something more like 30-35.

At the risk of oversimplification, an effective pass rush comes down to flushers and chasers. Texas had some of the former, but not enough of the latter. Flushers are players who can get initial penetration, displace the pocket, collapse a guard into the quarterback's face or get just enough initial heat to get the quarterback to move off of their spot. They don't have the ability to finish the play though. The quarterback flushes and runs away.

That's where chasers come in. Chasers feed off of the flushers. Chasers are hyper opportunists. They close distance and finish plays, taking advantage of the fact that the quarterback is no longer safe in the pocket, having abandoned the spot that their offensive line thought they were protecting. They run down the quarterback like a cheetah on a gazelle and finish the play with a sack, batted ball or strip fumble. They get all of the credit for the sack, which rightfully drives flushers insane, but a flusher without a finisher is like a great opening line without a closer. You're not getting that sale without either. It's also nice when a really talented chaser just runs around a flat-footed lineman for a sack fumble and suddenly the opposing offense has to keep their tight end or running back in for the rest of the game. Texas is starting to get chasers now and that should shore up the defense with better overall finishing ability, more negative play infliction and more turnovers.

Some of those chasers aren't just found on the edge – some of them, like David Gbenda and Anthony Hill – play linebacker.

LINEBACKER

Player	Height	Weight	Class
Anthony Hill	6'3"	235	SO
Liona Lefau	6'1"	225	FR
Ty'Anthony Smith	6'1"	220	FR
Davide Gbenda	6'0"	235	SR
Morice Blackwell	6'1"	220	SR
Derion Gullette	6'3"	235	FR/RS
Tausili Akana	6'4"	220	FR/RS

Anthony Hill was named the Big 12 Defensive Freshman of the Year after finishing 2nd on the team in tackles (66) and sacks (5) with 14 QB hurries. This season the dynamic true sophomore will move from his outside linebacker position to middle linebacker and the success of that transition will dictate a fair amount of the overall defense's efficacy. Hill will fill the shoes of the departed Jaylan Ford and though Hill is a better athlete than Ford, he will need to demonstrate Jaylan's instincts and steady tackling if the Horns want to field a consistent run defense. Hill got out of a run fit against Wyoming playing outside linebacker last year and it led to a long touchdown run. Hill doesn't have to demonstrate elite athletic ability to stop runs between the tackles, but he will need to understand angles and leverage and make the correct football play over and over. Part of middle linebacker is knowing when to seize the initiative and blow something up before it gets started or wait for the play to develop before making a move.

Middle linebacker is as much alchemy as science and the great ones study film relentlessly, but also play by feel and instinct. Hill has elite quickness and is the best blitzer on the team. He's sudden, refuses blocking, with motor and recovery in spades. From a coverage standpoint, Hill was pretty good in every game but Kansas State, where they exploited him (and frankly, the entire Texas coverage scheme) on crossing routes mercilessly, but that was more attributable to inexperience than inability.

He was an average run defender from an assignment standpoint and that's not unexpected for a true freshman. Notably, he went from an unreliable tackler early in the year to one of the best on the team by season's end.

Can Hill reliably play the run as a traditional linebacker inside? No one really knows until the bullets go live, but Hill is an outstanding athlete and hard worker who has shown improvement in every task that he's been charged with.

David Gbenda is a 6th year linebacker who has now appeared in 47 games with 11 starts. His return is big for the defense as his veteran leadership and experience at weakside linebacker allows Anthony Hill's move inside. David is optimistically listed at 6 feet tall, but he is thick and quick. After his playing time quickly slowed to a thick trickle in 2022, Gbenda showed real progress last year and he has gone from a marginal performer to a highly respected veteran and a guardian of the team culture. In previous years, Gbenda got caught chasing more ghosts than Ernie Hudson, putting him out of position and allowing offenses to run or throw the ball to his vacant space.

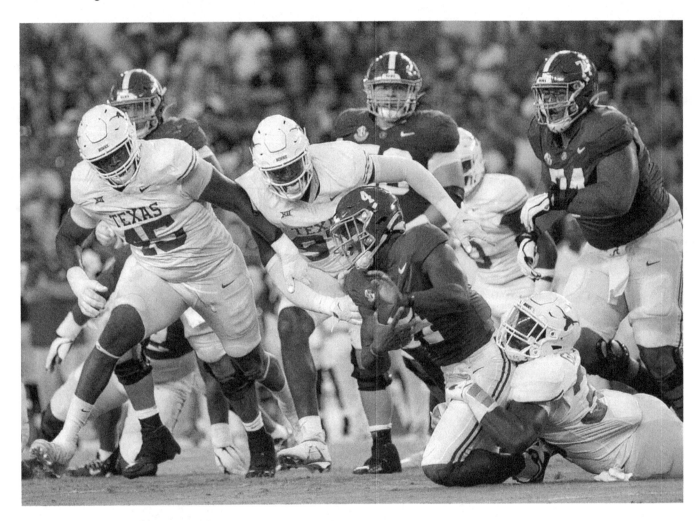

Continuity in the system and more time in a defined role has helped him considerably. Last season, Gbenda busted very rarely in the run game, was a reliable tackler and can be a voracious interior blitzer when his number gets called. His never-say-die attitude was embodied against Alabama last year when he was cut down on a blitz, popped up immediately to his feet and then sacked the mobile Jalen Milroe on a key 3rd down. That play was used by the coaches all season to demonstrate the energy and passion that they wanted from their defenders on every snap. Gbenda should embody that effort again in his 6th and final season.

Morice Blackwell is built like a safety but hits like a linebacker. The fact that he runs more like a linebacker is probably why he doesn't play safety. Often described as a dreaded tweener, Morice is comfortable in space and embraces contact, but it has taken some time for Blackwell to add the necessary weight to not get washed out by bigger athletes. He's now around 220 pounds after spending much of his career around 200. That should help his durability and ability to hold up to blocking. Blackwell played 187 snaps last year after missing the first three games of the season and he did see his play improve from quite poor to above average as the season progressed. He was more or less splitting snaps with David Gbenda at year end. The hard-hitting senior will be counted on to be a key reserve in a thin linebacker room, but coaches may slant his snaps towards certain spread-oriented offenses and throttle him back a tad against the bullyball practitioners. Blackwell has seen action in 37 games and it would be rewarding to see him emerge with a late career breakout.

Liona Lefau has good instincts and the requisite athleticism to be an effective off-the-ball linebacker, but he lacks a big frame and has struggled to put on weight. He has made it into the 220s now, which is good news. Lefau will back up Hill. He needs to get stronger, but his instincts and motivation to make a play are on point. Lefau has a reputation for being very opportunistic in pass coverage and it will be interesting to see if that translates on Saturdays.

Derion Gullette missed his entire senior season of high school due to injury and spent a good portion of a redshirt freshman season at Texas getting his body right. Gullette has elite athleticism but he still has to learn to play off-the-ball linebacker and we'll have a much clearer understanding of his role in August.

Tausili Akana was already 19 years old when he enrolled at Texas and the second year player has struggled a bit to add weight. That combo can be a bit of a warning sign with regard to potential ceiling. Originally slated as an edge, Akana is a natural pass rusher with good quickness and bend, but the staff will also try him at off-the-ball linebacker to take advantage of his movement skills and fill out a shallow depth chart. In addition to filling out the depth chart, Akana needs to fill out his body and it won't be clear what his real upside is until he's 235+.

Ty'Anthony Smith is a true freshman from Texarkana. He came in underweight, but he discovered the training table and added 20 pounds fairly quickly. Smith can run and has natural instincts for the position. Smith probably isn't physically ready to play yet, but he may be asked to do so anyway if the injury bug hits.

Prognosis

This unit can be very solid if Hill, Gbenda and Blackwell can remain healthy and play up to expectation – Hill has star potential – but there are too many question marks on the depth chart if Murphy's Law has any say. Injuries would devastate the unit more than any other position – defense or offense – and the gap between Texas' best linebackers and their backups is the most pronounced on the team. It is imperative that the offseason and some early non-conference games are used to build depth and narrow that gap. Liona Lefau would help the room by putting on some size and Derion Gullette is a good athlete but an unknown. UTSA edge rusher Trey Moore could get snaps at outside linebacker to bolster the unit (particularly in 3 linebacker sets) and get more talent on the field overall, but the staff's plans there won't be revealed until August or perhaps even September.

DEFENSIVE BACK

Player	Height	Weight	Class
Derek Williams	6'2"	195	SO
Jaylon Guilbeau	6'0"	190	JR
Andrew Mukuba	6'0"	190	SR
Malik Muhammad	6'0"	190	SO
Kobe Black	6'2"	200	FR
Jahdae Barron	5'11"	200	SR
Gavin Holmes	5'11"	185	SR
Jay'Vion Cole	5'10"	180	JR
Michael Taaffe	6'0"	195	JR
Xavier Filsaime	6'1"	200	FR
Jordan Johnson-Rubell	5'10"	190	FR
Warren Roberson	6'0"	190	FR/RS
Jelani McDonald	6'2"	205	SO
Wardell Mack	6'0"	190	FR
Santana Wilson	6'0"	190	FR

Jahdae Barron is a key returnee and the savvy veteran has 23 starts and 41 game appearances over his career. In his time at Texas, Barron has scored three non-offensive touchdowns, including a punt block return, a pick-six and a fumble recovery return. Barron has elite aggression, quickness and anticipation and he uses those attributes to terrorize both screen and outside running games to equal effect. His sheer aggression attacking those concepts is atypical for a nickel (Texas calls his role the STAR), but Barron's ability to recognize and blow those plays up is so profound that he has recorded 16 tackles for loss over his last 21 starts. Last year, he finished third on the team in tackles despite several nagging injuries over the course of the season. Barron is very good against the run largely because of his decisiveness, quickness and aggression and he is one of the best run-graded defensive backs on the team.

In the passing game, offenses targeted Barron 74 times, completing 44 for 476 yards. He also gave up two touchdowns and a season-long completion of 46 yards to go with one interception. That 6.4

yards per attempt mark isn't very efficient for the offense and holding opposing slot receivers to less than 60% completions and only two scores on the easiest throws on the football field is solid work. A healthy Barron can play better though and the next question is where? Jahdae is a good cornerback – some even believe he is better there than at nickel – and there is a legitimate debate as to whether putting Barron at cornerback with a new face at nickel makes for the best starting five in the secondary. That should be the defense's ultimate goal, particularly after a somewhat uneven performance from the pass defense last year. Additionally, while most college defenses spend their time in a base nickel, there are times when Texas goes to a more traditional defense and that takes the nickel off of the field. Does Texas really want teams to take one of their most dynamic players off of the field by virtue of their personnel grouping or would it be better to slide Barron to cornerback in those instances? Reasonable minds can disagree and whether he plays outside or inside will depend as much on the quality of his replacement at nickel as his ability to outperform the third best cornerback. So far indications are that Barron will remain at nickel, but the Texas coaches should not shy from experimentation.

Malik Muhammad had a terrific debut as a true freshman cornerback, forcing himself into the rotation at a position that was perceived to be locked down by veterans before the season. Muhammad's fine play can be credited as much as the veterans underperforming and opening the window of opportunity, but the young corner wasn't leaving once he made entry. Malik may have officially drawn only two starts over fourteen games, but he racked up 479 total snaps (which was 2nd among all Texas cornerbacks) and graded out as the best pass coverage defender of the lot. He also recorded 31 tackles and despite his slim build, physical immaturity and not getting the benefit of years of college level S&C, Muhammad was a respectable run defender, mostly because of sheer want-to and quickness. Malik takes football seriously and while he doesn't have elite gross measurables (other than long arms) his competitiveness, agility, skill base and anticipation are top tier.

The dexterous 6 footer is the best cornerback on the team and he might be the best defensive back overall. Enjoy his sophomore year because Texas fans will only get to see one season more.

Andrew Mukuba is a huge portal addition courtesy of Dabo Swinney's Clemson Tigers. At Clemson, the portal only flows outbound and the Horns are fortunate to be the recipient of a seasoned veteran defensive back. The Austin native was a three year starter for the Tigers (including starting as a true freshman) and over career 31 starts, he played at a fairly high level as both a traditional free safety and as a nickel racking up 149 tackles and 20 pass break ups over his career. That positional flexibility makes Mukuba particularly intriguing and it matches his physical flexibility on the field. Mukuba is extremely fluid and can adjust to the ball or man at an elite level without losing his footing or athletic base. Those "open hips" and his athletic efficiency are very useful as a deep safety or as a slot cover operating in tight space. He just doesn't get crossed up. Mukuba only has one career interception and whether that is a quirk of Clemson's schemes, a commentary on his hands, or indicative of an inability to complete the play is a bit of mystery. Mukuba is built lean and while he's a willing tackler, he can lose physical battles with receivers or running backs who are 25 to 40 pounds north of his playing weight. Acquiring a battle-tested veteran defensive back with outstanding positional flexibility is a real coup and Mukuba should be a vital piece in allowing Texas to get the best athletes on the field at every position in the defensive backfield. Mukuba is fully capable of playing nickel, but Texas might benefit most playing him as a deep safety with legitimate sideline-to-sideline range.

Gavin Holmes transferred to the 40 Acres from Wake Forest and after a season of acclimation and a healthy sprinkle of playing time, Texas hopes that this is the year that the senior cornerback breaks out. Holmes has long arms and good lateral quickness and the man coverage specialist also exhibits good change of direction and solid mirroring ability. From a developmental perspective, he's not very strong, can be sloppy getting jams at the line of scrimmage and that can compromise his ability to reroute and divert receivers. His weakness also compromises run support. The native New Orleanian played a great deal at Wake and when you combine his time there with last year at Texas, he has managed 42 game appearances with 16 career starts.

Holmes did see solid action last year, totaling 317 snaps. In those snaps, he was the 2nd highest rated cornerback in pass coverage on the roster per Pro Football Focus and is certainly one of the better pure pass defenders when Texas plays pure man coverage. Holmes doesn't have elite long speed or the strength to push bigger receivers off of their preferred line when he's on their hip, so it's crucial that he disrupts routes early and turns the battle into a contest of quickness rather than a pure speed game. In a game of slaps or tag, Holmes will win. In a game of pure horsepower, big and strong receivers can best him. The consequences of failing to get a good early disruption on a route were demonstrated in the Spring game when Isaiah Bond torched Holmes on a go route when Gavin guessed wrong on his jab and miscalculated Bond's anticipated release. It was a good lesson for Holmes and a correctable mistake. Holmes will compete for the starting cornerback job opposite Muhammad, but should be a valuable 3rd or 4th corner even if he doesn't win the starting gig. The more Texas plays man coverage, the more it favors Holmes' skill set.

Jay'Vion Cole was a late portal addition from San Jose State and the deeper one digs into the Cole mine, the more you realize that Texas may have found a neglected dirty diamond. A former two star recruit, the undersized and underrecruited Oakland native (Cole logged a 10.67 100 meters as a high school senior) was a lockdown cornerback in the Mountain West last year, holding his coverage victims to only 26 catches on 53 targets for 297 yards while surrendering 1 touchdown and intercepting 3 balls. He also had 10 pass break ups, which placed him 14th nationally. Giving up a sub 50% completion rate in modern football is quite good, but allowing only 5.6 yards per attempt and a season long catch surrendered of only 28 yards is the stuff of erotic fiction. A very specific coverage genre aimed at defensive coordinators, but let's not judge.

Cole's best strengths on film are his overall awareness and ability to split his focus between the receiver, the route combinations developing around him and the quarterback's release. He sees the field, not just the man. Most cornerbacks that attempt this and peek into the backfield fail miserably and surrender 70 yard touchdowns, but some gifted ones have layered vision. They can see everything all at once without suffering a migraine.

He particularly excels as a zone defender, though you also see these attributes on display when he's playing in off-man coverage. As for competition level concerns, they are valid, but the Mountain West had a few legitimate receiving talents (see UNLV's Ricky White and Boise State's Eric McAlister) and Cole also faced USC, Oregon State and 11-3 MAC champion Toledo in non-conference play. He knows what it's like to face quality competition and graded out just fine against the big boys. Speaking of grades, Pro Football Focus scored him a very strong 86.2 overall in 697 snaps, which was the 19th best score among cornerbacks encompassing 133 FBS schools. That's up from 59.6 in 2022 when he played at Cal-Poly, where he also snagged four interceptions before earning a portal upgrade to the Spartans' football program.

Can the undersized cornerback continue to scale up from FCS to FBS to SEC football? No clue! Texas staff don't really know either. However, there is objective evidence that Cole is on a massive growth trajectory and his soft skills are intriguing. Cole keeps solving increasingly difficult athletic puzzles every time he's asked to level up. Texas beat out the likes of Auburn and Michigan State (i.e. the 2023 Oregon State staff that went to East Lansing and remembered facing him in non-conference play) for his transfer, so Cole's upside wasn't completely off of the radar. Texas at least added quality depth, if not a starter.

Derek Williams arrived with major plaudits as an All-American high school recruit and he didn't disappoint as a true freshman, racking up 397 snaps and 42 tackles in the safety rotation while grading out 2nd overall to only Ryan Watts as a secondary run defender. Williams was also reasonably solid against the pass, particularly given his inexperience drinking from the firehose of college football. The tall and physical Williams certainly looked much more imposing and moved differently from the other safeties on the roster, but he may have taken his postseason weight loss a little too far, dipping under 195 pounds on his 6-2 frame. It would be nice to see Derek get back into the 200s.

Williams has good range overall but he is physical enough to drop down into the box, where his size and aggression can really be brought to bear. Williams is also good at supporting the run from depth.

Even from deep alignments, he gets downhill to contact with accuracy and no wasted motion; Texas hasn't seen a safety with that rare trait since DeShon Elliott. That valuable skill could allow the Horns to play two deep coverages without giving up too much in run support. Williams will be an important defensive mainstay, but whether he's the clearcut starter at one safety spot or part of a larger 3 or 4 man rotation remains to be seen.

Michael Taaffe is a fourth year junior and former walk-on from Austin Westlake who has 10 starts under his belt to go along with 27 appearances in his Longhorn career. As part of a multi-headed safety rotation last year, Taaffe compiled 48 tackles, blocked a punt and snagged three interceptions, which tied him for the team lead. Over 439 total snaps, Taaffe was an above average defender and he consistently exhibits good instincts and solid range from depth. It's worth noting that Taaffe's playing time increased as the season progressed. He averaged only 19.4 snaps a contest over the first five games of the season and 42.8 snaps per game down the backstretch. Taaffe garnered the most snaps of any safety on the team during that time period and that offers a fairly objective view of which player the Longhorn coaches thought best executed the defense and understood their role in it.

He's a willing hitter and the coaches like that he makes few mental mistakes. Taaffe also understands the larger defense well enough to coordinate the back end and get everyone lined up correctly. While fans tend to focus on pure physical traits (see departed safety Kitan Crawford), coaches understand that busted coverages hurt a defense more in modern football than minor physical inadequacies. Taaffe's weaknesses are generally overdone by casual fans while his strengths are ignored. Outside of a tough performance in only 18 snaps against Oklahoma (where he was not alone in disappointing – that game effectively ended Jalen Catalon's career at Texas), Taaffe was arguably the most consistent Longhorn safety on the roster. For that reason, Taaffe will see plenty of action in 2024, even with the arrival of Andrew Mukuba and the maturation of physical studs like Derek Williams and Jelani McDonald. Coaches have a hard time taking sufficiently athletic, smart players off of the field.

Jaylon Guilbeau is a third year junior from Port Arthur who has seen his Longhorn career unduly impacted by injuries. He impressed enough as a true freshman to start the first three games of the season at nickel before losing his job to Jahdae Barron and then missed the last five games of the season with a knee injury. Last year, he managed 134 snaps at nickel backing up Barron and he acquitted himself pretty well, seemingly growing more comfortable as the season progressed. Guilbeau is physical and competitive, but he is more quick than fast and there are questions as to whether he has the long speed to allow the Horns to play varied coverages when he doesn't have coverage over top. Guilbeau is an important depth piece who might see significant action with a strong Fall camp and potential shake-ups at nickel involving Jahdae Barron.

Jelani McDonald is a good enough athlete that he may have a forcing function on the staff's plans, even with some fairly clear hierarchies already established at safety and elsewhere. McDonald moves like an athlete twenty pounds lighter than his 6-2, 205 pound frame, but despite his size, the fluid sophomore has demonstrated the ability to potentially play any position in the secondary. If his weight gain continues, he might mess around and find himself as an elite coverage and blitzing outside linebacker. McDonald's early lack of a clear position is not due to a lack of fit to any one spot or being a "tweener" in the negative sense, it's that he projects pretty well to so many roles. Texas coaches are waiting for McDonald's body and overall comfort to declare where he's best suited. Right now, that's safety.

Warren Roberson impressed in the offseason as one of the most explosive athletes in the defensive backfield, but he's still learning the nuances of his craft. He will continue to find a lot of work on special teams and should battle for a starting job at cornerback in 2025 and beyond.

Kobe Black is a highly touted freshman who arrives with ready made size. He is already the largest cornerback on the team. Black could easily push to be the #4 cornerback, but Texas is starting to load up with talent all over the defensive backfield.

Santana Wilson, Jordan Johnson-Rubell, Xavier Filsaime and **Wardell Mack** are freshmen who will probably redshirt, but could earn the right to play on special teams. Filsaime and Mack had plenty of "Welcome to College Football" moments in Longhorn scrimmages, but they'll grow from it.

Prognosis

Since arriving in Austin, the Longhorn defensive staff has done a fine job upgrading the secondary through the portal (Watts, Holmes, Mukuba, Cole) while signing very strong traditional high school recruiting classes over the last two years. Their development of inherited talent has been a mixed bag. Far too many Sark-recruited older players – particularly from the 2022 recruiting class – plateaued, busted immediately, or actually got worse over time. That must be sussed out and addressed. Were these bad evaluations? Was it deficient positional development? Bad scheme? Simple bad luck? Nonetheless, the young defensive back talent on the roster is strong and after an extensive offseason purge of the defensive backs, the staff must strike the right balance between a talented youth movement and veteran leadership.

To put it bluntly, the Texas pass defense underachieved last year, performing as less than a sum of its parts in too many big games. On the season, Texas faced something less than a rolling ball of butcher knives at quarterback (Michael Penix and Dillon Gabriel excepted), but still surrendered 3561 yards passing at 7.1 yards per attempt along with 21 touchdown passes. In terms of overall passing efficiency defense, the Longhorns were a tepid 49th in the country, behind Iowa State, UCF, Texas Tech, Oklahoma and Kansas State – all teams that played the same league slate as the Longhorns, several of which could not match Texas talent overall. Without much change in personnel and despite adding another year of experience to multiple returning starters, the Texas pass defense was worse in 2023 than in 2022. That shouldn't happen and it revealed some individual developmental deficiencies and scheme breakdowns.

An absolutely dominant run defense made the overall defense appear much stronger than it was and teams smart enough to give up running and just chunk it around attacking certain flexion points of unit cohesion were consistently rewarded. Six different passers threw for 300+ yards against the Horns, to include a 378 yard performance from Houston's Donovan Smith (on 32 of 46 passing with 3 touchdowns and 1 pick) – which was his season best – and a 327 yard effort from Kansas State's Will Howard where he threw 4 touchdown passes and scorched Texas for 230 second half passing yards when the Wildcats stopped trying to run through a brick wall. That was also Howard's season high. TCU freshman Josh Hoover added his own 24 of 36 for 302 yard 2 touchdown effort. You get the idea. If your mental retort is that Texas shut down 3-9 Baylor's 2nd and 3rd string QBs, Wyoming's 2nd string QB in Austin, Texas Tech's injured starting QB and weak receiving corps and BYU's execrable passing attack, I can only bring a horse to water. You're free to pass up the refreshing spring of truth and guzzle all of the Cope-A-Cola you like.

New ideas and new blood were and are needed. Players and coaches. Clearly, Sark saw it the same way. He brought in former Arizona DC Johnny Nansen to help serve as a schematic idea man (the Wildcats were incredibly multiple and flexible under his guidance) to reinvigorate the defensive staff and better tie together coverage concepts on the 2nd and 3rd level while simultaneously clearing the decks on some experienced players – some of them multiple year starters – that the staff felt had consistently exhibited low football IQ and weren't getting better or were physically incapable of making the plays that the defense demands.

Texas flushed out eight defensive backs overall, several of them multi-year starters. From an outsider's perspective, that looks disastrous, but when one examines each player on a case by case basis, it is relatively clear who broke up with whom or, more charitably, where the parting was mutual. As a purely cold calculation, veteran players who can't play like heady veterans aren't worth starting over talented young players. The whole benefit of experience should be that you stop busting, forgetting defenses and ignoring coverage calls. Texas went to the portal strategically to fill in some gaps and now the remaining 2024 secondary is smarter on the field and probably more athletic overall. While some deep experience was lost, Texas still retains enough of it, even if some of that experience was acquired wearing another helmet with a Tiger paw or a Spartan on it.

That doesn't take the staff off of the hook. There were some bad game plans, mostly in the sense that there was no variation in game plan. Generally, a defensive coordinator does not feel comfortable trying innovative packages, fronts or wrinkles if they are not confident that the back end can dial in new coverages and "be right.". Apportion blame there as you wish, but the buck ultimately stops with Sark. The degree to which the staff can bring new ideas to a new secondary and get the best five out on the field will be the single greatest determinant of whether Texas fields a high level defense. Unlike last year, Texas won't have the gift of the most talented run stopping triangle in college football in Sweat, Murphy and Ford. That trio allowed shortcuts in so many areas. The defense's overall efficacy will in no small part hinge on the staff's ability to field an athletic deep secondary that plays smart cohesive football. Expect intense competition for starting jobs and rotation snaps will be earned rather than bequeathed. Muhammad and Barron are probably the only two returning starters who are "safe" though you should expect the staff to identify eight or nine players they're comfortable running with so that they can create a durable two deep meant to withstand the rigors of a potential 15 or 16 game schedule. Texas has legitimate depth across the board and must explore multiple combinations to solve the problem of getting the best five players on the field both individually and as a corporate unit. How an athlete plays in isolation is important. How he plays with others is equally important. The same can be said for the defensive staff's coaching.

This secondary must be headier and more cohesive if the Horns want to achieve their season ambitions. If they pull that off, Texas is a national title contender. If not, Texas fans should scale back their ambitions.

SPECIAL TEAMS

Player	Height	Weight	Class
Will Stone	6'0"	195	JR
Bert Auburn	6'0"	185	SR
Michael Kern	6'3"	195	FR
Lance St. Louis	6'0"	220	JR

Bert Auburn returns with the easy confidence of a white man with an afro and a prospective NIL deal with Pert Plus. Bert Plus returns with two years of experience under his hair net and is a collective 50 of 61 (82%) on field goal attempts over the last two seasons, including a 29 of 35 performance last year that made him the most prolific single season scoring kicker in Longhorn history. Over the last two years, Auburn is 16 of 21 from 40-49 yards and has never missed an extra point. Auburn is an elite kicker despite having only above average leg strength (though he has hit out to 54 yards), primarily because of his ability to reliably manufacture points in the key 30-49 yard area and his consistency on more routine kicks. At one point last year, Auburn hit 19 consecutive field goal attempts and finished the season 18 of 19 on any attempt below 40 yards. Longhorn fans welcome the return of one of the most reliable and proven kickers in Texas football history.

Will Stone handled kickoffs capably, earning 52 touchbacks on 94 kickoffs. When returners brought back his kicks, they averaged only a middling 20 yards per return. He also notched five tackles, serving as a reliable last line of defense. Stone averaged a solid 4.0 seconds per kick hang time, but if he can up that to somewhere between 4.2 to 4.4 seconds per kick, Stone will move from the top quintile of college kickoff specialists to the top decile.

Punting will be handled by 2024 signee **Michael Kern**. Texas will miss Ryan Sanborn initially, but Kern is a former high school all-state and All-American known for his efficient short set-up. The history of inexperienced punters at Texas is not glorious – at least in their first few debut games – but history shows that they settled in once the butterflies in their stomach shrank down from condor to hummingbird-sized. Expect Michigan to call for a punt block when Texas travels to Ann Arbor. If an inexperienced punter means that Texas is more likely to go for it on 4th and 3 at midfield, that's an exchange worth taking.

Longhorn coverage teams were quite good. They surrendered no points and very few meaningful plays. They particularly excelled in punt coverage. Texas held opposing punt returners to a measly 5.8 yards per return with a season long of only 18 yards and Malik Muhammad has a punt block touchdown against the Sooners in Dallas. Kickoff return coverage was solid, with opponents notching a season long return of 55 yards and just under 20 yards per return overall. Given the increase in athleticism and team speed over the last three recruiting classes, Texas should continue to see improved coverage teams. Keep an eye on players like Jelani McDonald, Tre Wisner, Warren Roberson, Michael Taaffe and Liona Lefau to head up this unit.

The Longhorn kick return game will transition to a deadly group of incoming transfers and homegrown talent. Matthew Golden, Silas Bolden, Johntay Cook and Jaydon Blue will be the headliners, but don't be surprised if a dark horse like Ryan Niblett or even Ryan Wingo assert themselves. It won't be at the expense of a healthy Matthew Golden though. Golden is the 2nd highest rated returner in college football and brought back two touchdowns last year from 98 yards (vs. TCU) and 100 yards (vs. West Virginia) on only nine returns. Texas will feature an elite return unit, particularly if Jeff Banks can identify some blockers willing to sell out.

Special teams are too frequently glossed over and while this preview does its best to emphasize their value, most of the ink is still devoted to the Texas offense and defense. The old saw that special teams are 1/3rd of the game, a wisdom often punctuated by the sound of dip spit into a filleted RC Cola can, isn't accurate. They're actually about 15% of the game, but that's a percentage of impact well worth your time and resources in tipping towards your favor.

Special teams – outside of individual kicker expertise which basically exists sui generis – are also a clear indicator of program attention to detail, total roster talent and general program aggression. Texas has scaled up on all three considerably. That's a great macro trend to follow.

Overall, special team coordinator Jeff Banks has done a fine job with the unit with Texas consistently ranking among the nation's elite. His units have particularly excelled in opponent negation: the blunting of the other team's big play special teams impact. That means no cheap points, big swings of field position or hidden yard advantages allowed. When the other team can't find any cheap explosives of their own, the game turns to offense and defense and the probability of an inferior team upsetting a superior one diminishes. Last year, Texas wasn't just about throttling the other team's specialty units, as they had some big plays on punt blocks (vs. Oklahoma) while scoring on a punt return (BYU) and kickoff return (Texas Tech), but the ability to negate the other team's efforts has been Jeff Banks' most consistent attribute of excellence. If Texas can get adequate performance from their punter and get a little better blocking on their return teams, they will do more than just thwart the other team, but create plenty of explosives of their own.

Ranking The 2024 Longhorn Football Schedule

As always, the pure quality of the opponent matters most in determining threat level, but road trips, rivalries, bye weeks, matchups and spots (i.e. where the opponent falls on the schedule) are material considerations. A tranche is more meaningful than a numerical ranking. There are four distinct difficulty groupings on the Longhorn schedule.

From easiest to hardest:

LEVEL I: BETTER WIN

Texas must sweep this group. Four of these five contests are at home.

ULM projects to be the only truly awful team in the group, but Texas will have marked advantages across the board against all of these teams. Mississippi State got a few players in the portal and Jeff Lebby outcoached the Longhorns last year as the Sooner offensive coordinator, but the Bulldogs aren't built to win in Austin. Vanderbilt is the only "road test" but the real test will be how many flights Southwest can schedule to Nashville the preceding Friday as Texas fans take over their stadium.

LEVEL II: THE MIDDLE CLASS

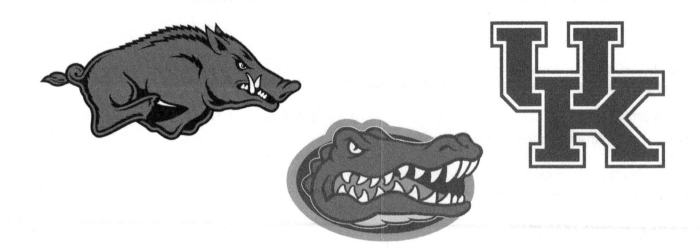

Arkansas makes it here because a road game in Fayetteville is meaningful and they have a new dual threat QB with some improv ability.

Florida has team talent, but they're playing Georgia the week before traveling to Austin with LSU, Ole Miss and Florida State immediately after. What a horrible spot for the Gators.

Kentucky is the early favorite for the middle tier team that plays Texas surprisingly well given that they're the week before A&M and after a potentially emotional road trip to Arkansas. The other reason? The Wildcats have more high end players than the average Texas fan knows.

LEVEL III: BITTER RIVALS WITH UPSIDE

Both historical rivals will play at minimum good defense. Upside rests on their respective offenses. Texas should be the better overall team in each contest, but both games are losable on the road or at a true neutral against opponents that can define their season with a win.

LEVEL IV: CHAMPIONS DIVISION

The defending 2023 national champion and the consensus projected 2024 national champion provide an interesting symmetry of challenge.

The Wolverines can't remotely hang with the Dawgs when you compare offenses, but the Michigan challenge posed to Texas is obvious: facing a dominant defense early on the road. If Michigan can rebuild its offensive line satisfactorily and find a quarterback, this is a true early test of quality.

Georgia is arguably the most talented roster in college football with a very good quarterback. Getting them after the Red River Shootout is brutal, but a home environment could compensate.

From a macro perspective, while it's obvious that Texas will face a much more talented slate in the SEC versus the Big 12 from week to week, Texas will no longer serve as the focal centerpiece for every opponent's program, university and general life validation.

Big 12 conference opponents used the Longhorns as their primary centerpiece for securing season ticket package sales, marketing to their fanbase, broader fundraising efforts and as a fan rallying point to act out their life's insecurities. It got a little old at times.

Don't believe me?

In 2019, University of Memphis professor Cody Havard, who studies fan behavior, told ESPN that his research showed that matchups with the Longhorns were frequently circled on the calendars of other teams' fans.

"We polled college fans and asked them who their biggest rival was," Havard said. "Texas has 11 different teams identifying them as a rival, by far the most in the country."

The runner up had three.

The SEC will represent a tangible psychological shift in that regard.

Texas still plays the Sooners in Dallas with road trips to Fayetteville and College Station – historical rivals that very much have Texas circled – but Texas as just another good opponent is the reality for most SEC opponents. That will only take deeper root over time as the novelty of Texas in the league wears off. SEC quality, passionate pre-existing rivalries, national and not regional ambitions and the big time feel of the league will distinguish the experience from Texas' prior peers.

The Big 12 was different. Even when the Longhorn program was comparatively weak – wait, especially when the Longhorn program was weak – opposing coaches and players still got full credit from their fan bases and administrators for Beating By God Texas. Even if that Texas team went 5-7. Beating Texas landed Big 12 coaches massive contract extensions, staved off firings and pretty much every Big 12 team considered Texas their primary rival. Longhorn fans were shocked to find out in their final Big 12 season that Iowa State players considered Texas their primary rival over Iowa. Huh? What? The number of Texas fans or players who have ever considered Iowa State a rival (considered them much at all) – zero.

The Beat Texas imperative was rife throughout the Big 12 and it became something of a crowdsourcing effort. Multiple programs dedicated April and August practice periods to specific Texas prep and would steal a day or two of preparation during another opponent game week in order to stay sharp for Texas three weeks hence. Multiple Big 12 staffs would share information with each other during their respective Texas game weeks. Working the phones with old coaching cohorts has always been a feature of football – "Hey, how did you guys approach dealing with their blitz?" – but multiple staff's game planning for one school as a crowd sourced project is another animal entirely.

To clarify: the All In To Beat Texas mentality is not why Texas fell off. Texas did that to itself with bloated stupidity and bad hires. This preview has documented that all quite thoroughly in years past. However, internal Longhorn decline enabled the All In To Beat Texas mentality. When every program in the league realized that beating Texas was actually an achievable milestone, "rivalries" suddenly sprang out of nowhere.

Rest assured that Georgia, Vanderbilt and Florida won't be doing group conference calls to talk about Texas. They've got other stuff on their plate. They don't view each other as co-conspirators in overthrowing the single team that defines their program validity. The SEC has its own bitter rivalries and plenty of other bullies to worry about. Beating Alabama, Georgia, LSU or Tennessee offers as much program relevance to Kentucky as beating Texas does.

Yes, the SEC will feature better teams, more talent, raucous road environments and a plenty of It Just Means More energy, but Texas won't have this odd asymmetry of perceived rivalry every week. Texas will always be a big game, particularly when any school hosts the Horns – it's a historically elite program that inspires strong emotions – but SEC schools host equally big games in other weeks against much more bitter rivals.

Let's talk about those games...

2024 TEXAS FOOTBALL SCHEDULE

	WEEK 1	AUGUST 31	AUSTIN, TX
	WEEK 2	SEPTEMBER 7	ANN ARBOR, MI
	WEEK 3	SEPTEMBER 14	AUSTIN, TX
	WEEK 4	SEPTEMBER 21	AUSTIN, TX
	WEEK 5	SEPTEMBER 28	AUSTIN, TX
	WEEK 6	OCTOBER 12	DALLAS, TX
	WEEK 7	OCTOBER 19	AUSTIN, TX
	WEEK 8	OCTOBER 26	NASHVILLE, TN
	WEEK 9	NOVEMBER 9	AUSTIN, TX
	WEEK 10	NOVEMBER 16	FAYETTEVILLE, AR
	WEEK 11	NOVEMBER 23	AUSTIN, TX
	WEEK 12	NOVEMBER 30	COLLEGE STATION, TX

Colorado State Rams
August 31 | Austin, TX

Head Coach | Jay Norvell

Key Losses | DE Mohamed Kamara, WR Justus-Ross Simmons, DT Grady Kelly

Key Additions | CB Isaiah Essissima, CB Elias Larry, TE Jaxxon Warren

2023 Record - 5-7

Former Texas assistant Jay Norvell enters his 3rd year in Fort Collins and the Rams have shown reasonable improvement during his brief tenure. At his prior stop in Nevada, Norvell transformed the Wolfpack from awful to respectable over five years (33-26 overall in his time there despite a 3-9 start) and the Front Range rebuild is going according to plan with Norvell leveling the Rams up from a 3-9 mark in 2022 to 5-7 in 2023.

Last season the margins were close. The Rams endured a double overtime loss to Colorado in a game that they controlled until they didn't, they suffered a 2 point loss to UNLV and an ignominious last second field goal walk off defeat by Hawaii. The Rams are close to playing winning football, but they will need more help in the trenches if they're going to consistently challenge the Mountain West elite. The halcyon days of head coach Sonny Lubick (6 Mountain West titles) and tough guy quarterback Bradlee Van Pelt spiking a football off of a Colorado defensive back's helmet while scoring a touchdown are not forgotten in Fort Collins (Colorado State, Van Pelt, head spike touchdown is worth the YouTube search), but the memories are growing dim.

The program is not without resources and commitment. The Rams boast a new stadium less than a decade old, state of the art training facilities and an attractive campus in a vibrant state. While the Rams have played good football in the past – most notably under former head coach Sonny Lubick – their most pressing issue is not a lack of consistent winning tradition, but compensating for their lack of a natural recruiting base and deflecting the steady incursion of big conference suitors wooing their talent via the portal and NIL. In the offseason, they lost two starting receivers and their best starting defensive lineman to programs like Syracuse, San Diego State and Florida State, with other key contributors departing for West Virginia and Florida.

That's the reality for Group of Five programs in the new era of college football and only the most creative, well-resourced and resilient programs will find a way to prosper and stem the outbound tide rather than just serve as a developmental farm affiliate. The Rams will be considerably outmatched in their season opener on the road in Austin (Las Vegas currently shows Texas favored by more than five touchdowns), but overall program improvement, a reasonable Mountain West schedule that features seven home games and hosting arch rival Colorado in Fort Collins suggests a team likely to break their six year bowl absence.

Strengths

The Rams have a capable passing game and like so many other programs nationwide, their lead trig-german is a former Texas high school quarterback. Aledo native Brayden Fowler-Nicolosi was pressed into action early when the Rams benched Clay Millen for poor performance in their home opener and they turned the reins over to the untested redshirt freshman for the rest of the year.

Despite his inexperience, Fowler-Nicolosi played well despite a penchant for turnovers. Brayden threw for 3460 yds to go with 22 touchdowns and 16 interceptions but he needed 470 pass attempts to get there for a middling 7.4 yards per passing attempt. His miscues came in spurts: he had four games with 2 or more interceptions. The Rams' quarterback is mobile in the pocket, but not a true run threat. His best attributes are fearlessness and accuracy under pressure. The young gun was bloodied and tested last year and should be much improved in his sophomore season.

This year, Fowler-Nicolosi will be even more comfortable in the Rams' quick spread passing attack, which asks the signal caller to make immediate reads and get the ball out quickly to a stable of talented pass catchers. Fowler-Nicolosi is a capable thrower (apparently bigger programs think so too – he was offered $600,000 to leave the Rams this offseason per Norvell) and their quick read, timing based passing schemes seek to isolate open men on the move via endless crossing routes – Houston and Kansas State nightmare flashback sequence initiated – and this will present an interesting unit challenge for the Texas safeties, nickel and linebackers.

The receiving corps is led by the lithe and deadly Tory Horton. The 6-2, 190 pound athlete has elite quickness and is a route runner par excellence, but don't underestimate his pure explosiveness – Horton was clocked at over 22 miles per hour against Colorado per Reel Analytics. Horton caught 96 balls for 1136 yards and 8 touchdowns last year. In fact, he's attempting to become the only wide receiver in Rams history with three consecutive 1,000+ yard seasons. His best attribute is his ability to create immediate space in the middle of the field on scrapes, slants, stops and crossers. His quarterback was an incredible 36 of 41 for 446 yards and 4 touchdowns when targeting Horton between the hash marks 0-19 yards from scrimmage. If Texas hasn't cleaned up that part of the defense from last year, it's a good bet that Horton will shine an uncomfortable light on it.

Though Colorado State lost their star tight end Dallin Holker to graduation and starting receivers Justus Ross-Simmons and Louis Brown in the portal, Norvell worked the transfer wire capably enough to bring in four native Texans to complement Horton. That's former SMU wide receiver Dylan Goffney (6-0, 215), former Texas verbal commit and Baylor Bear Armani Winfield and former Washington State and Cincinnati deep threat Donovan Ollie. Finally, former quarterback turned tight end Jaxxon Warren (6-7,

245) from North Texas State will bring raw athleticism to the position, but probably not much blocking. While the rest of the receiving group likely took a step back, Horton remains the straw that stirs the drink. Texas should gameplan for him to see double digit targets. In the first half.

The Colorado State defense wasn't a world beater last year but it featured a pair of fine safeties in Henry Blackburn and Jack Howell. Both are physical with high football IQs and the two returning seniors are more athletic than perceived. Howell led Colorado State with 114 tackles last year and was named 1st Team All Mountain West. He's an outstanding tackler and team leader, but he's questionable in single coverage. The more versatile Blackburn chipped in 75 tackles, 3 interceptions and 2.5 sacks to go with 7.5 tackles for loss. He also drew quite a bit of media attention (and death threats) for his aggressive hit on Buffalo standout Travis Hunter last year. Blackburn and Howell leverage their experience and physicality adeptly, but they are too often the saving tackle on a potential big play created by failures elsewhere in the defense. The Rams badly need to shore up the complementary pieces around them to have a defense at parity with last year.

Weaknesses

Last year, Colorado State's defense surrendered 29.6 points per game and just over 400 yards per contest, but they were capable of getting after the passer in spurts. That's despite a bend-but-don't-break pass defense that allowed opponents to complete an amazing 71.4% of their passes at a healthy 7.7 yards per attempt. The Rams pass defense was all too frequently bled out by endless nicks and cuts. Unsurprisingly, opponents converted nearly 44% of their 3rd downs and 56% of their 4th downs. Not giving up big plays and hoping for an offense to self-destruct is not a bad tactic against mediocre or inept offenses and the Rams held red zone visitors to 28 touchdowns in 48 red zone visits, but relying on opponent mistakes and a constricting field removes initiative and renders a defense nearly helpless against high executing offenses. It's also why they suffered a six minute deficit in time of possession last year. Teams could establish a lead and then play keep away with an endless succession of money down conversions.

The Rams will struggle to replace their best pass rusher in Mo Kamara (13 sacks, 5th round draft pick) and their best run stopper Grady Kelly transferred to Florida State. Their most dynamic returning defender up front is sophomore Nuer Gatkuoth, who is either a lanky edge or the name of a Dune villain. Colorado State has improved its depth up front overall, but most of them are bodies rather than impact players and they will be badly outmatched over four quarters going against the Longhorn offensive line. Quinn Ewers should be able to scratch off three lottery tickets in the pocket before having to pull the trigger.

A great deal is riding on new transfer cornerbacks Elias Larry (Navy) and Isaiah Essissima (Nevada) for this defense to blossom. Given that Navy and Nevada don't rate very highly as lockdown cornerback factories, the Rams are just hoping for adequacy. Colorado State's default coverage from their corners last year was lining up somewhere in Wyoming and their inability to play anything beyond soft man or a forgiving zone made their coverages predictable and put far too much playmaking responsibility on their fine safeties. Nickel Ayden Hector is competent and experienced, but this defense has little hope of tangible upside without the ability to challenge receivers outside on money downs.

The structure of the quick-throwing Rams offense is as much a necessity as a preference given the offensive line. Though Colorado State only surrendered 14 sacks last year, that statistic is deceptive. Fowler-Nicolosi releases the ball immediately to predetermined spots on timing routes. That's partially responsible for his inflated interception numbers but it also suggests an elite level of pass blocking competence that the Rams did not actually exhibit. This is a reasonable pass blocking unit, but the larger schematic and systemic minimization of sacks gives them a reputation they may not have fully earned.

Unfortunately, they might have earned their dubious reputation as run blockers. Colorado State offensive linemen exhibited little ability to get credible push in the run game, though they were certainly hampered by a subpar group of running backs for most of the season. On the season, the Rams averaged a measly 92 yards per game rushing at 3.3 yards per carry. The team was held under 100 total yards rushing on six different occasions. In frustration, the staff finally elevated 4th string 175 pound true freshman Justin Marshall over the last three games to change the dynamic and find some kind of spark. It worked. Sparks flew like an inoffensive Lifetime channel romantic comedy where the divorced chardonnay Mom meets the gruff handsome cowboy at the town corn maze. Marshall responded with 311 total yards rushing at 5.5 yards per carry with 119, 98 and 94 yard efforts in their last three games. Those three individual yardage totals were the best individual efforts of any Ram back on the season and the Rams exceeded 100 total team yards rushing in all three contests. Their likelihood of running the ball consistently against Texas are slim and none with Slim leaving town soon, but it is a trend worth mentioning. The Rams clearly found something in the diminutive Marshall and he'll be the starting running back in Austin.

Michigan Wolverines
September 7 | Ann Arbor, MI

Head Coach | Sherrone Moore

Key Losses | QB JJ McCarthy, CB Mike Sainristil, LB Junior Colson, WR Roman Wilson, DT Kris Jenkins, OG Zak Zinter

Key Additions | OG Josh Priebe, LB Jaishawn Barham

2023 Record - 15-0

B1G

Texas was an errant touchdown pass away from facing the Wolverines in the national title game, but alas that pass never came to pass. The 15-0 Wolverines defeated previous Texas opponents Alabama and Washington in the playoffs and won the national title behind the best defense in college football (10.4 points per game allowed), a stubborn running game and an early 1st round draft pick at quarterback with a penchant for converting 3rd downs. Seemingly nothing could derail the Maize N Blue championship train: not a massive cheating scandal for sign stealing, nor Jim Harbaugh's subsequent suspension, not All-American guard Zak Zinter's broken fibula, not even interim coach Sherrone Moore sobbing and dropping f- bombs on national television in a postgame interview after a victory over Penn State in which the Wolverines closed out the contest with 32 consecutive runs. Michigan wasn't always pretty to watch, but they were talented, focused, tough and incredibly well-coached at both the unit and position level.

The celebration didn't last long though. Not long after the ticker tape had been cleared from the streets, Michigan was rocked by the news of Jim Harbaugh's departure to sunny SoCal. The nine season head coach and lovable cheating maniac (86-25 at Michigan, three Big 10 titles) left for the San Diego Chargers along with his young elite defensive coordinator Jesse Minter. Six other key assistants, including Michigan's outstanding S&C guru Ben Herbert joined them. Michigan also lost 13 players to the NFL draft, the most of any team in college football. The Wolverines quickly elevated offensive coordinator Sherrone Moore to head coach and why wouldn't they? As the former interim, he boasts a spotless career coaching record of 4-0. The man doesn't know what it is to lose. The hasty elevation of an interim coach that the players love and demand has a time-honored and largely failed history in college and professional sports and it will be interesting to see if the inexperienced Moore defies the odds over time after the honeymoon period subsides.

Jesse Minter – who was arguably the best defensive coordinator in the college game – was replaced with coaching tree compatriot and former NFL defensive coordinator Don Martindale, who was once Minter's boss at the Ravens. Martindale taught him the system that Minter eventually modified to his own tastes and he is known for being far more aggressive than his star pupil. Martindale had elite defenses with the Ravens (three consecutive Top 7 in the league units) before his performance trailed off and he was fired in 2022.

Considering that the Ravens had some injuries, one bad year shouldn't lead to a firing, but John Harbaugh (yes, Jim's brother) had grown weary of Martindale's stubbornness, stale insistence on kamikaze blitzing every down and interference in areas outside of his purview. Martindale was hired by the New York Giants and they fired him after a year, partly due to insubordination to head coach Brian Diboll. Martindale and Minter share the same coaching lineage, so the core defense won't change too much, but Martindale does have a stubborn and uncompromising reputation that could cause friction with a rookie head coach. Martindale was the most aggressive blitzer in the NFL and there's a good chance that he will bring that approach to the Big 10, seeking to exploit college offenses with less sophisticated protections and inexperienced quarterbacks. Martindale's bag of tricks and disguises tend to run thin after an offense has seen them a few times, but the novelty and pure aggression of his schemes paired with Michigan's defensive personnel should prove a challenge for any team without the necessary components to jiu jitsu his aggression.

So after all of the personnel losses and the departure of most of their leadership and key developers – in some respects, an absolute gutting of the program – why are the Wolverines considered a top 10 team and a likely playoff participant?

Michigan brings back more than you might think on defense and despite their front line losses, they have been a development machine of late. They will have the best defensive line in college football and feature a cornerback who will be a top 5 NFL draft pick. That's not a bad base to start off a rebuild. Toss in a schedule that features only three or four meaningful challenges – Michigan gets to host Texas, Oregon and USC and travels only to Columbus to face the Buckeyes – who they have beaten 3 times in a row. Splitting those four games is not totally far-fetched. Their other games against teams like Minnesota, Illinois, Arkansas State and Michigan State don't inspire much fear in anyone. Michigan could fall off considerably and still be a 9-3 or 10-2 team. The negative case for Michigan is a bit more discerning. Their running game was actually dramatically overrated last year in every situation but short yardage, Sherrone Moore has proven absolutely nothing as a head coach, there's little reason to believe that losing their offensive line helps them run the ball better, the departed JJ McCarthy and a solid receiving corps (also largely gone) extended drives on 3rd and 9 constantly and the brilliant Michigan defense still keeps its major top line talent, but has some cracks in key supporting roles at linebacker and the secondary that it simply didn't have last year.

Jim Harbaugh has done this before and what happened after may be instructive. After he elevated Stanford from a West Coast doormat to bullies with high SAT scores, he left for the San Francisco 49ers with four key assistants (including coordinators Greg Roman and Vic Fangio) and left the inexperienced David Shaw in charge. Shaw went 54-14 over the next five years with four Top 10 finishes. Harbaugh *builds programs*, not one-offs. Of course, leaving Andrew Luck at quarterback will help any transition, won't it? Granted, Shaw's program eventually stopped running on Harbaugh's cultural fumes and he went 14-28 over his last four seasons before his departure, but Texas' immediate concern is with 2024, not with what the Michigan program might be in 2032. Harbaugh's DNA could remain in the Michigan program for years, but one must wonder if losing six assistants and arguably the best S&C coach in the game leaves Michigan more rudderless than the surface Sherrone Moore feel-good stories that permeate media suggest.

When you dig in, you find a team with some overwhelming strengths married to some major question marks. Styles make fights and if Michigan can keep contests centered on their strengths, it will be a long Saturday for their opponents. If they can't, the Wolverines will face a very different reality.

Strengths

Michigan will showcase the best defensive tackles in college football despite losing 2nd round draft pick Kris Jenkins. That's because Mason Graham and Kenneth Grant are absolute studs. The 320 pound Graham was the highest ranked player on Michigan's defense as of a season ago and he totaled 4 sacks and 18 hurries in 442 snaps, while absolutely shining as a run defender. His partner-in-crime Grant is a massive 340 pound anchor at nose tackle and while not quite as consistent as Graham, he's more explosive with 5 sacks and a ton of disruptive batted balls, hurries and pressures. Texas fans should understand the advantages afforded to a defense in having dominant defensive tackles and this pair is equivalent in terms of game impact to Texas' own 2023 duo of Sweat and Murphy. That should adequately convey what running inside will look like without some major scheming and deception to open up run lanes. Conner, Majors and Campbell should start eating their Wheaties now.

Michigan is also pretty darn good on the edge, though they probably won't boast 2023's waves of depth. Josaiah Stewart and Derrick Moore are disruptive players and though their numbers were suppressed last year by sharing snaps with NFL draft picks like Jaylen Harrell, their impact was still felt. Stewart transferred to Michigan from Coastal Carolina and he injected major athleticism at only 6-1, 245. He plays way bigger than his size and his brutal stuffing of Alabama All-American JC Latham, a man 85 pounds heavier, five yards backwards into Jalen Milroe's 4th down draw won a playoff game. McGregor has 21.5 total sacks over his career and he'll top 30+ by year end if he can avoid injuries. Derrick Moore looks like a NFL edge (6-4, 260) and has an elite first step. #8 flashes when he's allowed to let it go and the third year junior is seen as a potentially explosive breakout star who may be headed to the NFL after this season. It's tempting to believe that Michigan's new defensive coordinator will rely on a strong four man rush and cover behind them, but Martindale's history is to blitz additional players so that the four man rush can't be doubled and gets home more often and more violently.

There's more to like about Michigan on the periphery of the defense. Specifically, cornerback Will Johnson, who draws heady comps to players like Patrick Surtain. The 6'2" 200 Johnson enters his third year as a starting cornerback and he has already totaled 7 interceptions over his career despite being largely avoided in most game plans. In fact, Johnson intercepted a massive 8.5% of the passes targeted to his coverage and opposing QBs completed only 51.7% of their attempts against him over his career. Some shutdown corners preserve their stats with pass interference when beaten, but Johnson has had only five penalties called against him in 27 career starts. Johnson is dominant in man (he's the best pure man corner in college football) and pretty darn good in zone coverage as well. NFL draft boards have him as a Top 5 pick.

Michigan has a lot of questions and major losses on offense, but the tight end position is in good hands. Excellent hands, in fact. Colston Loveland projects as a high NFL draft pick and the 6-5, 250 pounder is still getting better. Last year, he grabbed 45 balls for 649 yards and was Michigan's best offensive player against Ohio State, while demonstrating good speed and tremendous body control. If the Texas staff game conspires to shut down any one component of the Wolverine passing game, it had better be Loveland.

Weaknesses

The Wolverine secondary features the best defensive back in college football in Will Johnson. Pretty good start for that unit. Another safety spot is secure with returning starter Makari Paige. So why a weakness, exactly? The rest of the unit should see decline after being ravaged by the NFL draft (they lost their boundary cornerback and nickel), the portal (lost starting safety Keon Sabb to Alabama) and injury (safety/nickel starter Rod Moore tore his ACL). That means the Wolverines now have questions at 3 of 5 spots on the back end. It's worth noting that the 6-4, 210 pound Paige is a big bodied tackler and solid defender when covering space and zone, but Michigan protected him with their elite coverage guys last year. The Wolverines are also replacing two traditional inside linebackers, both lost to the NFL draft. Their replacements are former starters at Nebraska and Maryland and it's not clear how they'll adapt to their coverage responsibilities in a new defense. Maryland transfer Jaishawn Barham is an elite athlete and blitzer, but he has a reputation for indiscipline in more conventional assignments. If Steve Sarkisian can get some throwing time for Ewers, the Horns can attack nickel-safety-linebacker cohesion inside and the corner opposite Johnson. If Texas can't protect Ewers against a withering pass rush, the new secondary may not matter all that much.

Michigan was cleaned out on offense, save a handful of players like Colston Loveland and explosive but often inconsistent running back Donovan Edwards. The Michigan offensive line goes from one of the most experienced units in college football to a patchwork, though a patchwork bound by strong unit level coaching and a good strength program. Not many blocking units can shrug off the loss of three draft picks and six offensive linemen overall, but if there is a program in the country that can pull it off, it's the team in Ann Arbor with a SMASH culture that has made it abundantly clear that their team is built from the offensive line out. Michigan program marketing and propaganda aside, there are good reasons to be skeptical, particularly about their pass protection. Their best solution may be to help the offensive line with simplified blocking schemes allowed by flooding the field with tight ends and running a very athletic QB.

They also lost a pair of underrated receivers to the NFL in Roman Wilson and Corn Dog Johnson. Wilson and Johnson were responsible for 74% of Michigan's receiver production and their replacements are unproven. There is a real path here for the Texas defense to gang up on the Wolverine run game, pay attention to tight end Colston Loveland and dare the Michigan passing game to beat them over the top.

What about that passing game? 1st round draft pick JJ McCarthy departed Michigan after amassing a 27-1 record as a starter. McCarthy didn't put up gaudy statistics, but he had a preternatural ability to convert 3rd downs and he had great command of the Michigan offense and its many checks in the running game. He made great plays, but mostly he kept Michigan out of bad ones. Now native Texan Sachse product Alex Orji has the inside track on the job pending the results of Fall camp. Orji is a 6-3, 235 physical phenom. He's ranked #1 in the Michigan program in their Key Performance Indicators for overall athletic ability – for example, he runs a sub 4.00 shuttle and has a 41 inch vertical. He's also an extremely powerful runner. According to Michigan practice reports, he's nearly impossible to take down in the pocket without a clean shot and he's a monster coming around the corner on the option. Who knew you'd have to gang tackle someone named Orji?

There's one problem though: no one knows if he can throw. In 2023, Orji had 15 carries for 86 yards and a touchdown, but no passing attempts. He threw one ball the year before. That isn't an inspiring track record and practice reports have been less than salutary for Michigan faithful. Can the former Sachse standout throw well enough to be a true dual threat? While inevitable comparisons to Jalen Milroe abound, Milroe throws most short and a couple of deep routes extremely well. No one has any idea what Orji can consistently execute in the passing game at the college level.

His most likely competitor is former 5 star QB Jack Tuttle who is in his 7th year of college eligibility (he was in the same recruiting class as 4th year NFL player Trevor Lawrence). The former Indiana transfer by way of Utah has started games in Bloomington and is a traditional pocket passer who would likely provide more passing game upside, but he missed the spring with a UCL repair. That's a blow to Tuttle's chances, but he'll still have a shot to stake his claim in August.

It's Orji's job to lose and Texas is probably the game where he either cements his hold on the job or the Wolverines are forced to explore other options. Preferably after his third interception to Malik Muhammad while trailing 21-0. Michigan loses a great deal on offense but given the departure of some key fixtures in the middle of the Longhorn defense, the Wolverines may just decide to shorten the game, ugly it up and see if they can push Texas around with Orji running it more than he flings it. Of course, that game plan requires neutralizing Sark's offense with the best defensive line in college football and an endless permutation of blitzes from former Ravens' defensive coordinator Don "Wink" Martindale.

Expect a contest of wills and contrasting philosophies in Ann Arbor.

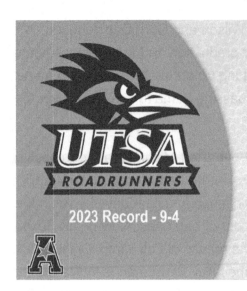

UTSA Roadrunners
September 14 | Austin, TX

Head Coach | Jeff Traylor

Key Losses | QB Frank Harris, LB Trey Moore, CB Kam Alexander, WR Josh Cephus, S Rashad Wisdom

Key Additions | CB Denver Harris, WR JJ Sparkman, C CJ James

2023 Record - 9-4

The Roadrunners finally say goodbye to Dr Frank Harris, the seven year quarterback who stretched his eligibility and the Roadrunner win column with equal skill during his time in San Antonio; the only quarterback in NCAA history to ever go from throwing touchdowns to collecting Medicare and earning senior rates at Sea World a week after his eligibility ran out. UTSA's very own Van Wilder remains with the program as a fundraiser and in his personal time he enjoys spending time with his grandchildren and napping on a barcalounger.

Harris started an incredible 52 games for the Roadrunners while throwing for over 11,000 yards and rushing for another 2,000+. More crucially, he was 39-13 as a starter (32-9 over his last three seasons) and came to define the never-say-die attitude of the program. Given that Jeff Traylor's career record at UTSA is 39-14, it does raise questions as to whether the Roadrunner program was built on Harris' perma-eligibility or Traylor's fiery coaching? Perhaps the answer is not monocausal. Why not both?

Aside from replacing the greatest player in school history, UTSA, like all non power conference schools, must deal with the reality of their roster being plundered by the big boys and being treated as a developmental rest stop on the hero's journey to the SEC and Big 10. UTSA digs for diamonds in the rough, polishes 'em up real nice and big school NIL bandits hijack them on the road to the NFL. Traylor and the city of San Antonio are battling that seeming inevitability with their own fundraising, by branding the 210 area code, shaking down local sponsors and relying on Traylor's tight knit culture built on maniacal effort, Tony Robbins style gridiron aphorisms and the judicious recruiting of hungry 3rd tier high school recruits mixed with elite program washouts seeking their last chance.

Traylor's program is encompassed by his Triangle of Toughness, which is admittedly similar to John Wooden's famous Pyramid of Success. He didn't copy it though! A pyramid is just a fancy polyhedron that's full of itself. The triangle is for the people. The percussion instrument of the common man.

Given Traylor's legendary East Texas roots, he made his philosophy a triangle since most East Texans have been burned by a pyramid scheme at least once in their lives and rightfully distrust its inherently exploitative geometry. "You mean I gotta pay up to you now? What the hell! I shoulda listened to Mama after all. That's Herbalife for ya!"

A further triumph of the Toughness Triangle is that Traylor fit eight different traits in a three sided object. He also managed to combine oddly specific advice like "Run The Football" with broad time-honored virtues like Integrity. Of course, like Traylor, enlightened TTF readers understand that Running the Damn Ball is its own virtue and not just a discrete game tactic. Many scholars believe that a lack of off tackle running has led directly to the growth of communism and men competing in women's sports wearing Capri pants.

UTSA will find a way to win. Even without their super-powered geriatric QB. That's what good coaches and good programs do and Traylor is a hell of a coach who has built something durable in the Alamo City. The Roadrunners won't win in Austin, but they will win plenty in the American Athletic Conference and, with a bowl victory, secure another season of double digit wins and move Traylor one step closer to a Power Four job.

Strengths

UTSA boasts a strong trio of running backs in Kevorian Barnes, Rocko Griffin and Robert Henry. Last year, the three combined for 1,786 yards rushing and 23 touchdowns. They're also capable pass catchers, totaling 42 receptions. Big runs were in shorter supply than the room's talent level suggests due to offensive line injuries, but with even adequate blocking the three should easily eclipse 2,000+ rushing yards combined while continuing to offer a reliable outlet in the passing game. Each has a distinct body type and running style, but the squatty Barnes (5-9, 220) is the most physical while Henry and Griffin provide the best big play potential. Expect the Roadrunners to pound the ball relentlessly to set up a play action passing game that should represent a departure from their "spread 'em out and let Frank cook" bias of the last several years.

The Roadrunners have some outstanding individual defensive personnel at nickel, linebacker and nose tackle. Brandon Brown is their best interior player and the former Tulane transfer is a high level run plugger who dominates the interior with pure strength and experience. He has 34 starts under his belt and already earned 1st and 3rd team All-Conference honors in '22 and '23. His anchoring is paramount for a blitz happy Roadrunner defense that totaled 46 sacks last year.

Linebacker Jimmori Robinson is a long (6-6, 235) and panther quick pass rusher and run blitzer who totaled 4.5 sacks, 11 tackles for loss and 10 QB hits last year. He's a capable blitzer inside, but he's also athletic enough to come off of the edge. They will need him to elevate if UTSA has even a faint hope of replacing the vital production that they lost with the departure of 2023 AAC Defensive Player of the Year and new Longhorn Trey Moore.

Nickel Donyai Taylor actually plays more like a hybrid linebacker. The 6-1, 205 athlete is an instinctive player who can stay in front of most slots at the G5 level, but is also capable of blitzing, holding the edge against the run and functioning as the 4th linebacker in UTSA's base 3 man front defense. He has terrific broad traits, but sometimes that can be exploited in an era of specialization. Unfortunately for UTSA, Sarkisian mercilessly exploited the big nickel methodology last year by hunting matchups in the slot and running off their support structures to get them in isolation. Taylor may be his next victim.

Weaknesses

The Roadrunners brought in transfer cornerback Denver Harris after tumultuous stops at Texas A&M and LSU and the former top 10 ranked state of Texas recruit could prove an interesting X factor. From one perspective, they got an elite athlete who might clean up his act and fundamentally change their defense. From another perspective, they were so desperate at cornerback after losing Kam Alexander in the transfer portal to Oregon that they are now banking on program poison to save them. The loss of four year starting safety Rashad Wisdom – their Frank Harris of the secondary – doesn't help the transition. While UTSA should be able to field a capable enough secondary, their likelihood of busting coverages and getting exploited over the top when they bring their blitz – a historical program weakness that was mitigated by Alexander and Wisdom last year – could re-emerge in 2024.

There's also uncertainty behind the center. Jeff Traylor will audition two QBs for the job replacing Harris: promising youngster Owen McCown and grizzled veteran Eddie Lee Marburger. Owen is the son of East Texas legend Josh McCown – a former 17 year NFL QB – and he has the inside track on the job if he can have a solid August camp.

The Roadrunners have a solid supporting cast for whoever wins the gig as they return most of their offensive line, some underrated receivers and eight overall offensive starters, but Traylor will have to make the classic decision between a literal Steady Eddie who minimizes mistakes but may not elevate the offense and a young maverick who makes as many "Oh whoa!" as "Oh nooo!" throws. McCown has legitimate star potential if he can put on some weight, sharpen his processing speed and better trust his natural feel. Both players saw action last year due to Harris' injuries and while the coaches clearly want McCown to win the job, Marburger is competing hard. So far, the more talented McCown has made enough mistakes in practice and scrimmages to keep it close.

Last year, McCown had a rocky early start in the Frisco Bowl against Marshall, but finished the game well, going 22 of 31 for 251 yards with 2 touchdowns and 2 picks. It was UTSA's first bowl win under Traylor. McCown also performed admirably when pressed into duty on the road against Tennessee, completing 18 of 20 for 170 yards in a 45-14 loss. For the year, he went 43 of 58 for 442 yards with 4 touchdowns and 3 interceptions, but he had a horrible spring game. Marburger is an established program veteran who also saw action last year, going 29 of 47 for 442 yards with 3 touchdowns and 4 interceptions. He was steady throughout the spring and showed command in scrimmages. If McCown performs well in August, the gig is his, but he has to win it.

The portal robbed UTSA of the chance of fielding Traylor's best ever defense in San Antonio. UTSA lost AAC Defensive Player of The Year Trey Moore to Texas. Then they lost standout cornerback and Frisco Bowl MVP Kam Alexander to Oregon, who will likely start for the Ducks. Both players are a testament to UTSA's recruiting and development, but a G5 defense can't simply shrug off the departure of two defensive superstars along with four year starter and field general Rashad Wisdom at safety and maintain their quality. The Roadrunners still have a number of fine players on defense, but the holes are big enough for a high level FBS team to drive through.

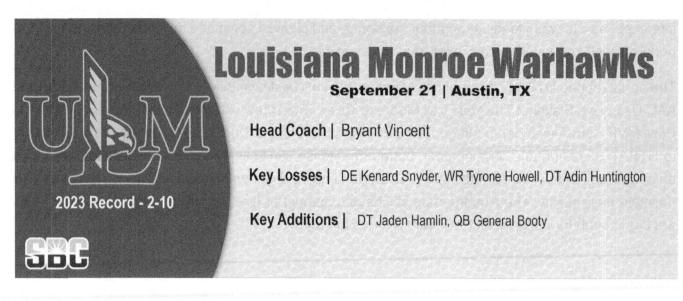

Louisiana Monroe Warhawks
September 21 | Austin, TX

Head Coach | Bryant Vincent

Key Losses | DE Kenard Snyder, WR Tyrone Howell, DT Adin Huntington

Key Additions | DT Jaden Hamlin, QB General Booty

2023 Record - 2-10

The Monroe Doctrine is the 19th century geopolitical tenet that the United States shall allow no interference from European powers in the Western Hemisphere.

The Louisiana-Monroe Doctrine is the gridiron proposal that the Warhawks shall not antagonize their neighbors by winning games nor establish any sphere of influence anywhere.

Since joining the FBS in 1994, ULM has had exactly one winning season and they have gone 6-6 four times. That solitary winning season occurred in 2012 – they went 8-5 – and it's referred to in their media guide as "The Magical Season." I'm not making this up. That season of enchantment was capped off by a 45-14 bowl loss to the Ohio Bobcats, but who are we to tell anyone what constitutes magic? That team finished tied for 2nd place in the Sun Belt and no one can ever take that away from them. Why has no one bought the movie rights?

"Men, lend me your ears. I want you to dig deep. As deep as the Saturday buffet line at the Golden Corral. If you believe in each other, we can be special. We can be...MAGIC. We could win 61% of our games and lose our bowl game by 31 points. Some say 'ol UL-Monroe can't win, but I believe we can attain a 2nd place conference finish! Now who is with me?!"

Before that, their most notable achievement was an early 1990s mascot fight between their Chief Brave Spirit and Northwestern State's Vic The Demon that can still be found on all-time mascot fight Youtube lists. Vic The Demon is a blue collar relatable demon who plays in a softball league and drinks Pabst Blue Ribbon when not tormenting mortals. The ULM mascot Chief Brave Spirit was from a time when they were still called the Indians, but were later forced to change their name not because of perceived insensitivity, but because local tribes didn't want their image associated with terrible football. Tribal elders offered ULM the opportunity to change their name to the Fleeing Squaws, but ULM correctly perceived this as a mean prank and they opted for the more intimidating Warhawks.

The Warhawks might want to stop picking fights and opt for peace. Wins have been scarce. The Warhawks are 10-36 overall and 5-26 in Sun Belt conference play over the last four years. That led to them finally firing head coach Terry Bowden, who was in the semi-retired, but still had name recognition, shamelessly padding-my-retirement phase of his coaching career. The Warhawks got worse, but Bowden probably paid off a beach house, so at least some dreams were fulfilled.

ULM hired Bryant Vincent to replace Bowden and he has his work cut out for him. Vincent has only one year of head coaching experience after serving as the interim head coach at UAB before being told to move on for Trent Dilfer. Getting chased for that goofball is a tough break, but Vincent went 7-6 with a bowl win during his UAB stint while Dilfer went 4-8 last year. Because the football gods have a sense of humor, the Warhawks will host UAB on September 7th.

The Warhawks have no winning tradition, were raided heavily in the portal for spare parts after last year's 2-10 debacle (which included 10 straight losses to close out the season), the city of Monroe and northern Louisiana have all of the disadvantages of the rest of the state without the great food and more fun-loving brand of corruption of their southern brethren and there's a good chance that they will start a quarterback named General Booty at some point during the season. The Warhawks should be terrible on the heels of a 2023 campaign that included 4 losses by 31 points or more and an 0-8 conference record. Their average score was a 35-17 loss and they lost by a combined score of 82-6 to Texas A&M and Ole Miss.

Las Vegas set ULM's 2024 season win total between 1.5 and 2.5 wins which means that a 3-9 season would be a cause for real celebration. Don't order the kazoos and party favors just yet, because 1-11 looks more likely. If that single win is over the Longhorns, Texas should probably cancel its football program and fire the entire coaching staff into the tower with a catapult.

Strengths

Did you read any of the preceding paragraphs? This team has no evident strengths. They have some passable individual personnel like running back Hunter Smith, guard Elijah Fisher and former walk-on undersized linebacker Carl Glass, but it would be a stretch to suggest any larger unit is particularly good and a deceit to emphasize any single player as worthy of specific game planning. The truth is that a bad team got worse across the board as most of their useful starters fled Monroe like a Kennedy brother at dawn. For what it's worth, ULM landed their first four star recruit in program history in JUCO defensive tackle Jaden Hamlin. Expect Hamlin to be an immediate starter and not to major in geography, because somehow this dude got lost on the highway driving to Baton Rouge, ended up in Monroe, and the coaches still haven't told him that he's not playing for LSU.

Weaknesses

Quarterback is a real problem for the maroon and gold. The anemic Warhawk offense averaged only 17 points per game and last year's three headed passing attack summed a paltry 6.1 yards per attempt while combining for 13 interceptions. This season the job appeared to be sophomore Blake Murphy's despite his rough freshman debut but he entered the portal in late March and still has no takers. That leaves 6-4, 225 Hunter Herring contesting Oklahoma transfer General Booty. Say what you will about Booty, but he is relatable at least. General Booty's name encompasses the closing time struggle of every college age male who began the night looking for specific ass, but must settle for general booty. Given that ULM went Booty hunting after spring practice and then added another transfer from North Texas for depth, it's clear that they believe that any Herring stinks when left out on the field too long. Not the case with Mike Trout though, is it? Whether they go Herring or Booty, there's something poetic in a moribund program starting the year at QB with an actual Red Herring or a man who would be Major Applewhite's commanding officer on a Monty Python Ministry of Silly Names org chart.

ULM had one of the worst pass defenses in FBS. They surrendered 28 passing touchdowns, 8.3 yards per attempt and 275 yards per game to opposing offenses. Their run defense wasn't quite as miserable, but the two primary stalwarts in that front are gone to Iowa State and Tulane. The Warhawks were 130th out of 133 FBS teams in yards per game margin and are at the near bottom of college football returning production with eleven starters from last year's team dissipated to the portal. Four of those eleven were starting offensive linemen. The Jawa from Star Wars couldn't have stripped them more efficiently for useful parts.

Mississippi State Bulldogs
September 28 | Austin, TX

Head Coach | Jeff Lebby

Key Losses | LB Nathaniel Watson, CB Decamerion Richardson, WR Zavion Thomas, CB DeCarlos Nicholson, DT Jaden Crumedy

Key Additions | QB Blake Shapen, WR Kelly Akharaiyi, WR Kevin Coleman, C Ethan Miner, OT Makylan Pounders, OG Jacoby Jackson

2023 Record - 5-7

Jeff Lebby has his work cut out for him in Starkville. The former Ole Miss and Oklahoma offensive coordinator and first time head coach takes over a 5-7 team that had its entire foundation capriciously dynamited by Zach Arnett, the in-house defensive coordinator who took over the Bulldogs head job after the tragic death of the great and colorful Mike Leach. The Bulldogs were returning a senior laden team that just had come off of a 9-4 season and a Top 20 finish. There was even irresponsible talk in Starkville that the Bulldogs might be SEC West contenders! At minimum, this was a bowl team and probably a .500 performer in SEC play. All Arnett had to do was keep the tires on the road and respect the system. Naturally, Arnett decided that Leach's untimely passing was his chance to rid Mississippi State of its timely passing and he scrapped the Air Raid entirely. The Bulldogs tried to transition to a power running football team despite their entire offensive roster being built around a system with pass blocking offensive linemen, no tight ends or fullback and a pure spread QB.

Terrific idea, Zach.

Never mind the fact that the Bulldogs had just put together 13 consecutive bowl appearances running asymmetrical offensive strategies engineered by the likes of Mullen and Leach and had learned the hard lessons that scheming against, rather than trying to pound, talent-laden SEC defenses was the way forward. The results were as predictable as they were brutal. Not only did they fail to run the ball, but they destroyed their passing game, throwing for fewer than 200 yards in eight games. Not only did Arnett destroy the offense (the Bulldogs averaged 12.6 points per game in SEC play) but a talented Bulldog defense was no great shakes either, allowing 37 points or more four times to SEC opponents. Arnett was fired with two games left in the season and the Bulldogs finished the year with a 1-7 SEC record.

Arnett is proof once again that not all defensive coordinators fail as head coaches, but the ones that fail all do it the same way.

Lebby's Veer N Shoot spread system will try to pick up the pieces, but Mississippi State ranks 122nd in returning production, lost three high level defenders to the NFL draft (including SEC Defensive Player of the Year LB Nathaniel Watson) and must engineer their offense back to the spread while weathering the natural rebuild on defense that would have occurred anyway.

It's not all dark clouds though. Jeff Lebby did a fine job of attacking the portal and brought in eight starters on offense that will form the core of the Bulldog attack. As for the defense? Well, maybe it will come along. But it won't. They will stink. The most bitter pill for the Bulldogs to swallow in rebuilding is that while they have the customary soft SEC non-conference schedule, they must face teams like Georgia, Texas, Ole Miss, Missouri, A&M and Tennessee in conference play. Starting the season with six guaranteed losses – several of them likely blowouts – is never heartening for any new staff. Jeff Lebby will create a functioning offense, but wins will be hard to come by for a team lacking infrastructure at so many key spots. A 6-6 record would be laudable overachievement, but 3-9 is legitimately in the cards.

Strengths

With veteran signal caller Will Rogers leaving Starkville, Lebby needed a QB. He needed an experienced quarterback looking for an opportunity who would find the town of Starkville impressive. Naturally, he looked to Waco. Blake Shapen, the 23 year old transfer from Baylor, will bring maturity and extensive starting experience to Jeff Lebby's Brilesian offense. Shapen's starting record (10-13) belies the fact that he played well for Baylor last year before his injury and a nearly 3:1 career TD/INT ratio speaks to his growth over time. He's an above average college QB who actually fits what Lebby wants to do philosophically and he can be outstanding in the RPO and play action staples that are the core of Lebby's system. Shapen isn't explosive athletically, but he is very coordinated and can throw from different platforms on the run. Shapen is also barely 6 feet tall, so Lebby will continue to use the Dillon Gabriel permutations of his pass protection and pocket set up to allow him to operate.

If Shapen can stay healthy, he will be a stabilizing force and should allow the Bulldogs to play very competently on offense against any opponent that can't just overwhelm them at the line of scrimmage. Expect Mississippi State to be in more than its share of shootouts against middling opponents, but if the Longhorn offense brings their A game, Shapen should be playing from behind for most of the contest and the Longhorn pass rush should make his game day experience in Austin very exciting.

Mississippi State fans breathed a sigh of relief when they found out that the Miner that Lebby had been secretly contacting on the internet was of the UTEP variety. Phew. Close one. UTEP wide receiver Kelly Akharaiyi is a 6-1, 200 pound elite deep threat who totaled 1,033 yards receiving on only 48 catches last year. His 21.5 yards per catch ranked near the top of all FBS receivers and his downfield skill set is perfect for Lebby's system. Akharaiyi does have a well-earned reputation for drops (12.1% of all catchable balls) but his penchant for 65 yard touchdowns tends to compensate. He's complemented by Louisville transfer Kevin Coleman, who was a former 4 star recruit who caught 26 balls for the Cardinals last year. Coleman will occupy the slot and should be their highest volume pass catcher overall. Jordan Mosley will be the only homegrown pass catcher and Mississippi State fans think that he's potentially a future stud. Behind them, Lebby signed three four star freshmen wide receivers, so the future is bright for their pass catchers. One player likely destined for greatness is Mississippi State backup wide receiver SanFrisco Magee. Regrettably, the roster does not have a Chu-cago Jones or Nuyorc Jenkins, but a man can dream.

The Bulldogs also added the Ball brothers from Vanderbilt and Buffalo – a pair of 6-6, 250 pound tight ends who excel as blockers and are capable enough in the red zone. They will be incorporated heavily into the running game but should also serve as additional pass protectors when the Bulldogs try to hit Coleman and Akharaiyi deep on play action.

Weaknesses

The best possible upside for the Bulldog offensive line is borderline competence. The potential downside – particularly with an injury or two – is disaster. They lost every starter from last year's team and will replace them with four from the portal and a former JUCO transfer. Their new starters at center and left tackle are experienced, but they come from Memphis and North Texas (center Ethan Miner has 36 career starts and was highly graded in Denton, at least). The new guards come from Power Four programs, but Texas Tech's Jacoby Jackson was a rotational player in Lubbock on a less than stellar offensive line and LSU transfer guard Marlon Martinez was on the bench in Baton Rouge. Finally, right tackle Leon Bell has never started and only appeared in games at Kilgore JUCO. The group won't lack for size and Lebby's offense is pretty offensive line friendly, but this unit could struggle not just from an individual talent standpoint but also as a cohesive whole learning to deal with new line rules and wide splits that help to create natural running creases, but also expose offensive linemen to slanting and gapping from more athletic defensive linemen. Lebby's offense doesn't require dominant offensive line play to flourish, but all offenses require a minimum qualifying amount of solid play across all five positions in order to stay ahead of the sticks. It's doubtful that the Dawgs will be able to hold up against higher end defensive lines and the SEC has plenty of those.

The defense is going to be pretty bad. Mississippi State lost eight defensive starters, three to the NFL and a couple more to the portal. First-year defensive coordinator Coleman Hutzler will face a major challenge in finding sufficient starting talent and depth while also installing his take on the 3-4 system. Hutzler will start several transfers who were either marginal starters at other FBS programs or struggled to find much playing time overall. Players with that profile don't have a great track record of breaking out. They lack pass rushers and they are not good enough in the secondary to compensate with blitzing without paying a heavy price. Both starting cornerbacks are inexperienced, with one of them now playing for his 4th school. To upgrade, they have their hopes pinned on a rotational West Virginia transfer that missed most of the last year due to injury. 6-3, 200 pound safety Corey Ellington is the brightest spot on the defense and he is likely to lead the unit in tackles. They need about six more like him to be league average.

Jeff Lebby is a good hire, but Starkville is as much a description of what he inherited as his new residence. While he has done heroic work in the portal and on the recruiting trail to bring in legitimate skill players, key infrastructure on offense and defense is lacking and Mississippi State needs more time to recruit it in and build it out.

Oklahoma Sooners
October 12 | Dallas, TX

Head Coach | Brent Venables

Key Losses | QB Dillon Gabriel, OG Cayden Green, OT Walter Rouse, OT Tyler Guyton

Key Additions | WR Deion Burks, C Branson Hickman, DE Caden Woullard, DT Damonic Williams, OT Michael Tarquin, OG Febechi Nwaiwu

2023 Record - 10-3

Brent Venables rebounded in his second year after a rough 6-7 inaugural season. The Sooners won ten games and their season zenith was a thrilling last second win in the Cotton Bowl over their primary rival. Their inability to handle secondary rival Oklahoma State or a scrappy Kansas disallowed a Big 12 title game rematch with the Longhorns and sent them to the Alamo Bowl, where they lost 38-24 after allowing Arizona to score 25 straight points to close out the game. That 10-3 mark was Oklahoma's 19th double digit win season since 2000 and it restored a great deal of confidence in Sooner fans and players. Winning games engenders belief and beating Texas is ecstasy, but a highly favorable schedule may have created a bit of a mirage. Oklahoma was not as bad as their 6-7 record in 2022, but they probably were not as good as last year's 10-3 suggests either.

Massive turnover on the offensive line, a new quarterback, a new offensive coordinator and a far more challenging schedule might reveal that the Sooner rebuild is still a work in progress. A strong SEC schedule means that Venables will have to prove that he can get the Sooners up for quality opponents that aren't just wearing Burnt Orange and the Sooner habit of stealing extra practice days for Texas from other opponent prep weeks is much more dangerous than it used to be. Last season, the Sooners played a forgiving schedule ranked 37th nationally in difficulty. This year they will face a slate projected as the 7th hardest in college football. That includes the annual Red River Shootout against Texas, which is preceded by a road trip to Auburn, hosting Tennessee, travel to Ole Miss, LSU and Missouri and hosting Alabama. They have their typical patsy non-conference slate, with a depleted Tulane representing their best challenge, but the SEC schedule certainly delivers some worthy opponents. If Oklahoma goes 4-4 in SEC play and then takes care of business elsewhere, an 8-4 record would be nothing to be ashamed of and would defeat preseason Vegas expectations that placed their season win total at 7.5. Of course, if Jackson Arnold is as impressive as Sooner fans hope he is and he proves to be a superstar, all bets are off.

Oklahoma has new coordinators on both sides of the football. On offense, expect a slightly new direction. On defense, expect better alignment. The new defensive coordinator is an extension of Venables' beliefs and philosophy. 30 year old Zac Alley will be the titular head of Brent Venables' defense, but the key phrase there is Brent Venables' defense. Alley is schematically aligned with Venables (Brent is his mentor and Alley worked for him at Clemson) and he'll allow his head coach more leeway to coach the whole team as well as specifically game plan certain opponents. Prior defensive coordinator Ted Roof wasn't really a fit and Alley is described as a "mini-Venables." So now the Sooner sideline will have two men stalking it who look like they overdosed on Nicorette gum. Before coming to Oklahoma, Alley did a great job at Jacksonville State, helping Rich Rodriguez lead a first year FBS program to a 9-4 record. Alley is default aggressive. Like Venables, he will blitz anywhere on the field and generally his best idea to counteract a team that beats his blitz is a different type of blitz.

Offensive coordinator Seth Littrell replaces new Mississippi State head coach Jeff Lebby as the Sooner play caller and while Oklahoma will remain committed to the spread, Littrell's lineage is Air Raid rather than the Brilesian Veer N Shoot. Though Littrell's DNA has plenty of Mike Leach in it, the former fullback loves the running game and he's also adopted some Brilesian concepts of his own. A couple of his offenses while at North Texas were jokingly referred to as the Run Raid, but he is a pragmatist who tends to play the cards he is given. One of the most tangible changes that Littrell will make is to Oklahoma's offensive pace. Lebby was an unapologetic proponent of the hurry-up no-huddle and Oklahoma's goal was to go as fast as possible to limit defensive substitutions, attack defensive conditioning and short circuit sideline adjustments. The problem is that the increased play load also wore down the Sooner defense and rapid 3 and outs brought to mind the old military adage "Never hurry to your death." Littrell will hurry it up situationally, but Oklahoma will move from being one of the fastest paced offenses in the country to something much more moderate.

Like Texas, Oklahoma will face an upgraded schedule, novel teams, better talent and challenging environments. They will find out a true picture of where the program really is. So far Brent Venables has done a laudable job remaking his roster inheritance from Lincoln Riley via the portal and recruiting trail but you should remain skeptical that the Sooners are restored just yet.

Strengths

Sooner offensive explosiveness will be considerably raised by two new faces. One is new to the team, the other is a Sooner runner new to the top of the depth chart. Purdue transfer Deion Burks was the star of spring practice and he'll replace Drake Stoops as the starting slot. He scored two touchdowns in the Spring Game and he has high level quickness and a knack for playmaking after the catch. Burks will be WR1 and shutting him down will be key to stopping the Sooners. The other Sooner wide receivers range from just-a-guy to above average (Jalil Farooq, Nic Anderson), so Burks will be key for them. The other new face will be running back Gavin Sawchuk. He was the best pure runner on the team last year, but inattention to detail and spotty blocking limited his chances. He still led the Sooners in rushing (120 carries, 742 yards, 6.2 yards per carry, 9 touchdowns) and the 5-11, 195 pound runner has outstanding vision and cutback ability. He is a capable enough receiver (14 catches last year).

Backup Javontae Barnes is a standard issue FBS runner so keep your eyes on standout freshman Taylor Tatum from Longview. He's a dude.

Oklahoma has a great pair of defensive backs in Billy Bowman and Peyton Bowen. Bowman led the Sooners with six interceptions last year and he's a tremendously instinctive athlete who makes plays from sideline to sideline. Bowman plays bigger than he is and he sees the game with clarity. Sophomore Peyton Bowen earned over 350 snaps last year as a true freshman and acquitted himself well. He's an elite athlete and he's comfortable in the box, lined up at nickel or playing as a deep safety. They also have the flexibility of playing big Robert Spears-Jennings, a 220 pound safety who brings the boom in the running game and plays pass defense acceptably. The flexibility of this room will allow the defensive brain trust to get different combinations on the field matched to the opponent.

Linebacker Danny Stutsman is the soul of the Sooner defense. He had 104 tackles, 16 tackles for loss and 3 sacks last year in addition to several clutch plays that aren't adequately captured by the box score. Stutsman is at his best when blitzing or shooting a gap and he's good at redirecting on the move, but he is just above average as a pure off-the-ball diagnostician. Like any good Sooner, he is at his best when he is cheating before the snap. Sooner media and fans love to trumpet the athleticism of his compatriot Jaren Kanak. His athleticism is undeniable but it is often headed in the wrong direction or whiffing very athletically on a tackle (he missed 22% of his tackle attempts last year). Kip Lewis is scrappy and undersized and missed over 17% of his tackles. Lewis probably has the best chance of leveling up instinctively, but all three Oklahoma linebackers are at their best firing downhill on a game console tied to Brent Venables' intuition. When Brent guesses wrong or they are asked to play base defense facing a diverse offense, the preseason magazine touted "strength of the defense" is actually a weakness.

The Sooners have a deep edge room. No single player is elite, but they have several plus performers and a veteran or two that can be mixed and matched depending on opponent strength. They brought in All-MAC Caden Wouillard from Miami (OH) and the 6-4, 260 edge has 26 career starts. Last year, he had 9.5 sacks for the Redhawks and was one of the more coveted Group of Five transfer options. The perma-eligible Trace Ford returns for his 6th season and he fills the role of established veteran who understands what to do. Ethan Downs had 4.5 sacks for the Sooners last year and he is on a solid developmental trajectory. He has filled out to a solid 6-4, 265. Finally, PJ Adebawore is a physical freak still growing into his lanky body, but he is one year closer to marrying high level athleticism to more physicality and on field awareness. He may have the highest upside of anyone, but if he isn't ready for prime time, the Sooners have plenty of other options. Speed rusher R Mason Thomas rounds out the group.

Weaknesses

Sooner offensive line coach Bill Bedenbaugh must replace all five starters on the offensive line. A group that combined for 4,188 collective snaps in 2023. Bedenbaugh has done a terrific job since being hired in 2013, but one must wonder how an elite offensive line coach got caught with his pants down in consecutive seasons such that the Sooners needed five portal transfers to provide three starters and two key backups. This isn't new. In 2023, the Sooners started transfers from Stanford, Cal and Appalachian State. How does that happen? Fortunately for the Sooners, Bedenbaugh has always been gifted enough at his craft that he is still able to squeeze out acceptable performance from a makeshift bunch. It works… until it doesn't.

Let's discuss those transfers. 6th year senior left tackle Michael Tarquin is at his 3rd stop (Florida, USC, Oklahoma) and he has compiled 18 career starts in his wanderings across the college landscape. Tarquin was fine at USC last year, but saw his season truncated by injury and then USC told him he would have to fight for his job this year with a talented youngster. So Tarquin hit the road. North Texas guard Febechi Nwaiwu was a nice grab. He has 19 career starts and earned major plaudits as a freshman, but last season was cut short by injury. He's a big physical monster and the Sooners need him to lock down a guard spot. Center Branson Hickman from SMU has 35 career starts and he will be a smart, stabilizing force. He is agile and technical, but lacks ideal size. The Sooners also added Michigan State's Spencer Brown (23 career starts) and he will battle for the job at right tackle or serve as the primary backup. Washington guard Geirean Hatchett will be a key backup who does have some limited starting experience.

Oklahoma is really counting on two home grown options to step up in order for the line to come together. Jacob Sexton was a below average player last year at tackle, but he should play better at guard this year. Right tackle Jake Taylor will battle Spencer Brown for the right tackle job. He already has the inside track despite no career starts. Whether that's a commentary on how promising Taylor is or how bad Michigan State's offensive line was last year remains to be seen. How quickly can Oklahoma establish a viable starting five? How cohesive will they be? Can they weather injuries? These are the important questions that must be answered satisfactorily if the Sooners want to field a dangerous offense. If the questions are not answered, a new system, a struggling offensive line and a young quarterback can become a volatile combination.

No player in college football has more preseason variability potential than sophomore quarterback Jackson Arnold. The Sooners needed to or wanted to (depends who you ask) go to Jackson Arnold over Dillon Gabriel because Gabriel's high floor could not be selected over Arnold's potential ceiling. They sure as hell could not afford to keep both. The highly touted five star could legitimately be a Heisman finalist...or a turnover machine that the Sooners have to protect and scheme around. The preview flipped a coin and decided to describe his traits under the weakness column, mostly because he is a question mark under live fire and his bowl performance suggests that for all of his talent, he may not be quite sure where to go with the football yet.

The 5 star from Denton (the 7th highest ranked recruit in Oklahoma football history) had his starting debut in the bowl game against Arizona and his 399 total yards (361 passing, 38 rushing) and three interceptions were a box score bottom line that appropriately demonstrated both his upside talent and recklessness. Arnold matched some incredible intermediate throws with some seriously misguided ones, but he demonstrated elite velocity between the hashes and terrific athleticism. The talent is clear, but decision-making was opaque. The mental side should progress with more reps and time under tension, but the Sooners probably wish he had a more supportive offensive line situation and more dominant receivers outside to help nurse him through his growing pains. Arnold is a strong situational run threat – and he has gained weight up to around 215 pounds to enhance durability – but his run game will likely be limited to keep him healthy and keep backup and former Longhorn Casey Thompson (now on his 4th university, the guy just loves education) holding a clipboard. Jackson Arnold will put up massive numbers against some early non-conference scrubs, but wait until the heart of SEC play before making any judgements.

The Sooners and various preseason magazines love to talk up cornerback Woodi Washington and his 36 career starts. Not this one. The fact that he's entering his 6th year at a position that the NFL lusts after is your first clue. The analytics agree. Last year, he was targeted more than any Sooner defender in the passing game. Opposing quarterbacks hit 39 of 65 balls for 606 yards with 4 touchdowns and no picks on Washington. The next worst Sooner defender gave up 329 total yards. Leaving aside pure volume, on an efficiency basis Washington conceded 9.32 yards per attempt and 15.5 yards per completion. If a QB did that to every defender on the field, he would have a good shot at the Heisman. Every corporate preseason magazine touts him as a major strength and "a lockdown cornerback", but the data and film disagree. His counterpart Gentry Williams was better and Gentry will punish mistakes (3 interceptions) but opposing quarterbacks still hit 66.7% of their passes on him, though nearly entirely underneath. Kendel Dolby – who can play nickel and cornerback – was their best player at keeping the ball from going over his head and the Sooners should play him at their nickel extensively. Their other primary backup outside is San Diego State transfer Dez Malone. He was OK, but it is worth noting that he was worked over a bit by the higher end Mountain West passing games. It is hard not to love the Sooner safeties, but the Sooner cornerbacks are the place to attack.

Georgia Bulldogs
October 19 | Austin, TX

Head Coach | Kirby Smart

Key Losses | OT Amarius Mims, DE Marvin Jones, LB Jamon Dumas-Johnson, TE Brock Bowers

Key Additions | TE Ben Yurosek, RB Trevor Etienne, WR Colbie Young

2023 Record - 13-1

You know a program is used to breathing rarefied air when a 13-1 record and a #4 AP final ranking is considered a disappointment. The Bulldogs lost the SEC title game 27-24 to Alabama and failed to make the playoffs after winning consecutive national titles despite a late push by media who argued that the defending national champions must be allowed to defend their title in place of Big 12 champion Texas (who conveniently had a win over Alabama) or in lieu of the Alabama team that had just beaten them head-to-head. That line of reasoning is what happens when you teach an entire society to think in terms of narratives, but here we are. The Bulldogs were left out of the playoffs and had to console themselves by humiliating Florida State 63-3 in the Orange Bowl, facing Tallahassee frat guys and some migrant workers from a Home Depot parking lot that the Seminoles suited out when all of their mercenaries decided to opt out.

Last season doesn't change the fact that Georgia is the top dog in college football – they have won 2 of the last 3 national titles, boast a 42-2 record over the last three years and they haven't lost a regular season game since 2020. The only two losses over their last 44 contests have come in SEC title games to Alabama and they were able to avenge one of those in the 2021 national title game. Given a choice, that is the correct title to win. Last year, they won their average game by 25 points and often their greatest opponent was their own boredom. They actually struggled with middling teams like South Carolina, Georgia Tech and Auburn, but showed their true class when focused and motivated by blowing out Ole Miss 52-17 and smacking Tennessee by four touchdowns in Neyland. On the season, they averaged 7.3 yards per play to their opponent's 4.8 for an outstanding +2.5 delta. For comparative purposes, Texas was a very good +1.5 in that metric (6.7 vs. 5.2) but that's not within sight of Georgia's mark in terms of down-to-down dominance.

Why is Georgia so good? A combination of elite talent, high level resources, top notch individual development and pretty darn good game day coaching. Nits can be picked here and there – their offensive game plan against Bama last year was something they would like to run back and they beat Ohio State in 2022 with a heavy dose of good luck after CJ Stroud carved up their defense – but no one accuses Kirby Smart of just rolling out the football and letting superior athletes run around randomly to victory. They coach it up pretty well and Georgia does not remain static from year to year. One of Kirby Smart's greatest attributes is that while he is a former defensive coordinator, he does not build his team around "protecting his defense." The Bulldogs are actually a much more explosive passing team than conventional wisdom suggests and they frequently bring aggressive offensive game plans to big games. Going 94-16 over 8 years and upending Nick Saban as the SEC's alpha bully is testament to that fact. The other testimony? A ten year, 130 million dollar contract. The final piece of evidence? Smart's ability to wear a visor during night games and no one calls him an asshole for doing it. That is real power. They... just let him do it. Kirby should wear footie pajamas and a sleeveless leather vest against Clemson in the opener just to see if anyone will dare to call him out.

Georgia shapes up as the best and most well-rounded team in college football. However, unlike previous years, they face a much stiffer schedule than what they are typically accustomed to enduring. Adding Oklahoma and Texas to the conference fold had a brutal ripple effect on seemingly every SEC schedule but Texas A&M and Missouri. The Dawgs open early against Clemson in Atlanta and travel to Tuscaloosa, Austin and Oxford. Hosting Tennessee is no layup either. Texas and Alabama on the road replacing South Carolina and Missouri is a serious step up and Georgia faces the very real prospect of dropping a regular season game like normal teams do. Of course, their opponents face the very real prospect of seeing a focused Georgia that reminds everyone of why they are the consensus preseason #1.

Strengths

Carson Beck is the most proven pure passer on the Longhorn schedule and a guaranteed 2025 high 1st round NFL Draft Pick. A consensus of NFL scouts project Beck ahead of Ewers, but there is a lot of football to be played and preseason lists aren't worth much absent final season data points. That caveat written, I tend to agree. Beck is more consistent over more types of throws. Before the 2023 season, the 6-4, 220 pound Florida native beat out the guru-anointed 5 star Brock Vandagriff for the starting job in August (Vandagriff eventually transferred to Kentucky) and Beck played quite well for the Bulldogs, giving them one of the most explosive offenses in school history, ranked 3rd in the country by advanced statistics FEI. Beck threw for 3941 yards while completing 72.4% of his passes and added 24 touchdowns to only 6 interceptions. Georgia's loss to Bama in the SEC title game can be pinned on a conservative offensive game plan more than anything Beck failed to do (Beck was slicing and dicing Bama until the Dawg offense mysteriously retreated into a shell for two quarters and then decided to go back to Beck when it was too late) and Georgia's 40 points per game scoring average would have been even higher had the Dawgs embraced pace and leaned more on their greatest strength: Beck's arm and decision making.

Beck has a solid arm and is a decisive pocket passer who keeps his eyes downfield, ignoring the pass rush swirling around him. His 9.45 yards per attempt average and 13 yards per completion are a testament to his ability to get the ball down the field. He rarely makes unforced errors (only 1.4% of his pass attempts were intercepted). Beck is not a runner, but he is maneuverable and can credibly buy time when needed. Carson is certainly not perfect – sometimes his feet get crossed up and he can overstride. Nor will you confuse him with Ben Roethlisberger – he's not shrugging off a free pass rusher. He can also be overly risk averse and his effectiveness declines if you can move him off of his spots. He is a conventional quarterback who thrives in a good system. He is not a chaos agent that "creates." He lets the talent around him do that.

Beck has one rare attribute at the college level – he throws receivers open. On intermediate stop routes, the ball gets out with so much zip and accuracy to the correct shoulder (meaning the opposite shoulder of the closest defender) that the receiver is able to create after the catch while the defender is still in recovery mode.

Georgia added former Gator running back Trevor Etienne this offseason and he will add an important element of explosiveness to their running game. The 5-9, 200 pound Etienne has already run for over 1,400 yards at 5.7 yards per carry over his freshman and sophomore seasons and he is an elite make-you-miss-guy – tacklers miss 27% of their attempts on him. As good as Etienne is as a runner, the idea of Georgia using him consistently in the passing game is somewhat terrifying.

Georgia also has strong receiver talent. Dominic Lovett, Rara Thomas and Dillon Bell form a quality trio and Miami speedster transfer Colbie Young was the rave of Spring practices. Georgia spreads the receiving load around (UGA has not had a 1,000+ yard receiver since Terrence Edwards in 2002) so no one player will put up gaudy numbers, but in aggregate they are not a pleasant group to face. An agnostic offense that just throws to the open guy. Georgia lost a once-in-a-lifetime tight talent in Brock Bowers. Naturally, they replaced him with elite blocking tight end Oscar Delp and jump ball specialist Stanford transfer Ben Yurosek, who picked Georgia over Texas. Georgia loses a 1st round tight end and replaces him with two mid round NFL draft picks. Poor, poor Bulldogs.

Finally, the Georgia offensive line profiles to be strong. They return four starters and their new center Jared Wilson has drawn quality early reviews. The unit particularly excels as pass blockers, but both guards are plus run blockers. Earnest Greene should be a star at tackle by mid year. Georgia has ten legitimate players on the two deep that they are happy to play and the drop off from starter to back up is negligible. This is the deepest offensive line in the country, but if you want to find something to criticize, no single player is as good as Texas' Kelvin Banks.

Georgia edge Mykel Williams is a 6-5, 265 4.5 40 utter freak who has finally matured into his body and skill set. The SEC coaches voted him 2nd team All-SEC last year despite Williams missing some starts and rotating early in the year. Based on his trajectory, a few NFL scouts believe that he will be the 1st selection of the NFL draft. That is quite bold, but it gives you some idea of his ceiling. Picture a supersized Will Anderson. Inside, Warren Brinson and Nazir Stackhouse are NFL quality players and Georgia rotates them with some upside guys like Jordan Hall and Christen Miller. None of them are Jalen Carter level elite, but we are talking about four future NFL players here. The Dawgs weren't dominant inside last year, but this stage of development is when Georgia interior players historically grow into their contract year and break out.

Do the Dawgs have a good secondary? Indeed. Safety Malaki Starks will be a NFL 1st rounder and he's incredible against the run from any depth. Georgia can line him up 20 yards deep and he still fits the run like he is 20 feet from the line of scrimmage. Starks will also cover: opponents averaged a pathetic 5.7 yards per attempt on him and he punished those attempts with 3 picks and 7 pass break ups. Corner Daylen Everette is also quality, but his traits have thus far exceeded his play. Georgia has a very good record of play catching up to traits and they're counting on that hitting with Everette this year.

Weaknesses

If there was a relative weakness with Georgia's team last year, it was a defense that ranked 11th in national FEI after consecutive #1 finishes in 2022 and 2023. As Texas fans will learn this year, there is a gap between quality defensive tackles and dominating monsters. Kirby Smart believes in stopping the run with the least number of defenders possible so that they can devote that extra manpower to coverage and prevent single play explosives. It is a great philosophy when your linebackers and front are dominant, but when they are not, you get run on a little bit. That creates some breakdowns in the larger defense. These are relative criticisms of course – Georgia gave up 15 points per game and had a top 8% defense overall. But that isn't the top 1% to which they are accustomed. Georgia is so accustomed to defensive dominance that when offenses do work them over a little bit, they can lose composure and make more mistakes.

Georgia must replace 3 of 5 starters in their secondary. They will count on a pair of absolute stud 5 star freshmen – Ellis Robinson and KJ Bolden – to play significant roles at cornerback and safety. Steve Sarkisian will certainly respect their raw talent, but also see them as an opportunity ripe for exploitation with double moves, play action, sucker plays and a lot of sneaky Sark mischief. Inexperienced talent in the secondary makes plays when allowed to rely on instinct and just read and react, but Texas is going to try to make them read, read again, question their read, pause that reaction and then watch Isaiah Bond glide past them into the end zone. Could a little panic set in with guys trying too hard to make up for a mistake in front of a hostile crowd of 105,000? You bet.

Georgia's well-roundedness (every unit on their team is arguably a Top 10 unit nationally) and general lack of personnel or schematic weakness is irritating, but Texas will bring a motivated crowd and a smart game plan in Austin. Expect a slobber knocker.

Vanderbilt Commodores
October 26 | Nashville, TN

Head Coach | Clark Lea

Key Losses | WR Will Sheppard, WR London Humphreys, DE Nate Clifton

Key Additions | QB Diego Pavia, WR Loic Fouonji, TE Eli Stowers, OG Steven Hubbard

2023 Record - 2-10

Vanderbilt's black and gold represent two key elements of their football program. The gold represents the television contract wealth that the private school exchanges to serve as the league's sacrificial lamb while contributing viewership and media impact comparable to Northwestern, while the black represents the permanent marker ink W-I-N that every opponent marks next to Vandy on their pre-season schedule. The Anchor Down motto also tells you something about Vandy's philosophy in the SEC football regatta. "You guys brave the waves, we'll hang out here and have some umbrella drinks." The Vanderbilt formula is well established: take the loss, take the fat check, hire a new coach in four years who will sell the alumni on how it can all be different, do some capital improvements, rinse, repeat.

That may read a tad cynical, but this is a program that has had five winning seasons since 1975 and six winning seasons since 1956. Things are not trending great in Nashville for 4th year head coach Clark Lea either. After a promising but deceptive 5-7 finish in 2022, there was wild talk of the Commodores qualifying for a bowl game on the strength of their returning starters and a wide receiver room that many programs envied. Instead, they went 2-10, lost every SEC game by double digits and their three best wide receivers all portaled out. Vanderbilt had the sixth worst offense in college football and the second worst defense by EPA (Expected Points Added). Put simply, Vanderbilt underachieved versus low expectations play by play, not just on a seasonal basis. Their 2-10 record did not hide some secret level of competence – their wins came against Alabama A&M and a 35-28 nail biter against Hawaii in Nashville. In response, Lea fired most of his position coaches, demoted his defensive coordinator and brought in New Mexico State offensive coordinator Tim Beck (no, a different one) to revamp the offense along with transfer quarterback street fighter Diego Pavia

If you squint your eyes hard enough at a relatively favorable schedule, a 4 win season is possible. If Vanderbilt can win a couple of SEC games, it would be cause for real celebration but it is hard to find a potential upset victim. Diego Pavia will give them a will to win and that's a start.

Strengths

The Commodores have a new quarterback: New Mexico State tough guy Diego Pavia. He's exactly what they need, less from a skillset standpoint, but definitely in terms of attitude. If you made a list of players who would not belong at preppy, collar-popped, private school Vanderbilt, he would be at the top of the list. The appeal of Pavia for a program that too often plays beneath its admittedly modest talent levels and has a tendency towards baseline complacency is that Pavia plays football like his life depends on it. Like a contest of Aztec Pok-a-Tok – the ancient Meso-American contest where the losing team was frequently executed.

He plays with a tree stump on his shoulder, not a chip. The former New Mexico state champion wrestler and state champion quarterback had major offers from multiple wrestling powerhouses, but he chose to stick with football despite zero interest from major programs. After a stint at a military prep school, Pavia got a reluctant offer from the New Mexico State Aggies. The 5-11, 200 pound Pavia doesn't look like a QB, doesn't act like a QB (he urinated on rival New Mexico's field; he double legged and body slammed an Auburn defender that intercepted one of his passes, precipitating a near bench clearing brawl in New Mexico State's upset blowout win at Auburn) and he doesn't throw like a QB – his throwing motion often resembles a European trying to scare away a raccoon with pine cones – but his niftiness in the pocket, running ability, ability to change levels to avoid tacklers and knack for hitting timely big time throws dragged the Aggies to 17 wins over the last two years. That's no small feat. New Mexico State is a program with a 35% historical winning percentage and a historical 0% belief in itself. Pavia played a big part in changing that.

His production is undeniable. Last year, Pavia ran for nearly 1,000 yards and threw for another 2,973 with 26 touchdown passes to 9 interceptions. More amusingly, he attempted 68 deep balls, only hit 21 (a 31% completion percentage), but those passes went for 788 yards and 8 touchdowns. Even when he's grossly inefficient, he's still winning. He's also a winner in another sense. His underdog teams won 70% of the time against the spread. So even when New Mexico State lost, they did it above expectation. Pavia doesn't have the polish or NFL potential of most of the quarterbacks that Texas will face, but he will fight for 60 minutes with both fists bloody. That's an attribute that Vanderbilt sorely needs.

Weaknesses

Vanderbilt's best three receivers transferred out to Georgia, Colorado and Boston College, enervating the only real unit strength on last year's roster. They did add New Mexico State tight end Eli Stowers and he will be a primary target for Pavia, but this will be the worst receiving corps in the SEC. That's unfortunate, as Pavia's improvisational skill and willingness to throw high risk/high reward balls would have worked with these departures well. Running around like crazy to buy six seconds and then chucking it downfield does not make for an efficient offense, but it's not a bad plan for a team looking to upset superior teams.

Vanderbilt can't run the ball. Last year, Vandy averaged only 95.3 yards rushing per game at 3.3 yards per attempt and they were ranked 125th in run explosives. They converted only 33% of their 3rd downs and less than 30% of their 4th downs. Though their quick passing game didn't surrender many sacks, Vanderbilt's offensive line allowed 100+ hurries. The Commodores will embrace a spread option rushing attack and Pavia provides a legitimate extra man advantage as a ball carrier, but do they have the horses up front? They brought in a pair of portal transfers inside to solidify the line from Mississippi State (he's pretty good) and UTEP (he's not) but their homegrown returnees are below average and right tackle will be manned by a sophomore with no game experience. Vanderbilt will compete with Mississippi State and Arkansas for the unenviable title of Worst Offensive Line In The SEC.

Head coach Clark Lea – a former defensive coordinator at Notre Dame – takes over the Commodore defense. There is room for improvement here given that they surrendered over 36 points per game. Opponents averaged 5.1 yards per carry and they were the 101st ranked defense in college football by FEI advanced metrics. Opponents completed a healthy 69% of their passing attempts at 8 yards per attempt and added 26 touchdown throws. Add it all up and the defense surrendered 6.5 yards per play and was ranked 129th overall in passing efficiency defense. Lea will get Vanderbilt out of some stupid calls and deploy assets better overall, but where are the playmakers? Safety CJ Taylor is the only one really worth a mention. The Commodores will improve on offense by virtue of having a winner like Pavia under center and an offensive coordinator with a pulse, but the defense has little upside and they won't be able to control games the way they need to in order to impose their preferred style.

Florida Gators
November 9 | Austin, TX

2023 Record - 5-7

Head Coach | Billy Napier

Key Losses | WR Ricky Pearsall, DE Princely Umanmielen, RB Trevor Etienne, OG Micah Mazzccua

Key Additions | WR Elijah Badger, WR Chimere Dike, OT Brandon Crenshaw-Dickson, S Asa Turner, CB Cormani McClain

The football gods and the Southeastern Conference schedulers hate Billy Napier so very, very much. Here's why:

Miami

Samford

Texas A&M

@ Mississippi State

UCF

@ Tennessee

Kentucky

Georgia (neutral)

@ Texas

LSU

Ole Miss

@ Florida State

Florida plays eight preseason ranked teams. Four are preseason Top 10 teams and they play all four of those in succession. After that murderer's row on the back half of the schedule, their reward is a ranked in-state rival on the road for their season finale. Road games at Florida State, Texas, Tennessee are brutal and a neutral vs Georgia is no walk in the woods either. What about their gimme wins? Well, we can pencil Samford in the win column and you can sell me on the road game at Mississippi State, but dangerous unranked teams like Kentucky and UCF are not to be confused with Grambling and Wofford. UCF head coach Guz Malzahn loves to game plan the hell out of one marquee opponent every year and you can bet that they will do that for the Sunshine State's marquee state university. As for Kentucky, read this preview. They have some dudes and if their transfer QB pans out, the Wildcats are a problem.

Billy Napier needs to win now, but the Gators face the hardest schedule in college football. If the goal is 7-5 or 8-4 – which would certainly make them a Top 15 or Top 20 team by any sensible power rankings – they must deliver victory against all the teams that they should beat and then pick off Texas A&M and LSU at home and take down Miami or Florida State. That's not impossible for a talented but uneven football team, but this squad also lost five in a row to close out 2023. If things go sideways again this year, the Gators could conceivably open up a big can of quit over the back half of the season as the portal vultures circle over Gainesville. Florida starts some studs next to negligible players and it takes real coaching and finesse to overcome those chinks in the armor and keep an opponent's blows landing on your shield and not the vitals.

Is Napier capable of real coaching under intense pressure? He won at Louisiana Lafayette by stockpiling superior talent to his Sun Belt competition, developing well and then winning close games despite often playing down to his competition. Is that replicable to the SEC in a short window? The Florida Gators have had three consecutive losing seasons and Napier is a smooth 11-14 in his two seasons in Gainesville. Winning 44% of your games at a school that sits in the best recruiting grounds in the country with tremendous resources and a supportive administration that has won three national titles since 1996 is not going to cut it. Particularly when new Florida president Ben Sasse has been publicly frank about his belief that winning football is imperative to enriching the student experience and ensuring alumni giving. Napier has recruited very well and is selling the long view of program building, but in a college football world dominated by portal transfers, NIL and recruiting wars no one is stockpiling patience or grace for their multi-millionaire head coach.

Strengths

No 2023 preseason transfer was met with more eye rolls and chuckles than failed Wisconsin thrower Graham Mertz's move to Florida, but Mertz had an overlooked renaissance under center despite the 5-7 Gators disappointing record. A player who once threw 4 interceptions in a single game against Notre Dame and 26 total picks in his previous starts for the Badgers, threw only three interceptions (with 20 touchdowns) the entire season and proved to be an efficient, mistake-free leader for a deeply risk-averse Gator offense that played covered in bubble wrap. These are strange times when we put the 23 year old Mertz in a strengths column for anything other than hair or politeness, but the Wisconsin transfer who set back quarterbacking several years in Madison was objectively good for the Gators, nearly throwing for 3,000 yards, albeit in very small increments. Mertz very rarely tested defenses downfield, but he proved accurate and efficient in a tempo short passing game that allowed him to complete over 70% of his passes and average a respectable 8.1 yards per attempt. Mertz may not have outright won many games for Florida – one can look to the Florida defense and in-game coaching to explain why – but he never played a really bad game all season and his touch and timing in the short game created yards after the catch on the regular.

The next evolution for the 6-3, 220 pound athlete is to take his 40+ career starts and a promising 2023 and build new skills. A little bit more downfield, please. 69% of Mertz's passing attempts were 9 yards down the field or less and his 6.7 yards ADOT (Average Depth of Target) was amongst the least field-expanding of all college football quarterbacks. If some passers arc wild gunslingers, Mertz is more of a pepper spray and a whistle on a cord around his neck type of fellow. If the Longhorn short passing game defensive woes that were exposed last year aren't cleaned up, Mertz and Florida's core competencies will reveal it. Mertz is backed up by native Texan and 5 star physical phenom DJ Lagway. If the Gator season begins to falter, they won't be shy about throwing in the 6-3, 240 pound freshman, even if Mertz is not at fault for the losses. Either of them will have sufficient targets. The Gators lost stud receiver Ricky Pearsall to the NFL, but they love sophomore Eugene Wilson (61 catches, 6 touchdowns as a freshman) and Arizona State transfer Elijah Badger (65 catches last year) is a strong complement. Chimere Dike from Wisconsin rounds out the trio and he was the Badgers' leading pass catcher in 2022.

Florida has the potential for a solid offensive line if left tackle Austin Barber can stay healthy and if transfer right tackle Brandon Crenshaw-Dickson from San Diego State steps up. He notched 35 career starts for the Aztecs so experience won't be an issue. Despite the Gators' 5 yards and a cloud of dust passing attack, they surrendered 39 sacks last year. The blame can be equally divided amongst Mertz, who has a tendency to take sacks instead of throwing it away, a scheme poorly suited to converting long third downs, and the play of an offensive line working its way through injuries. However, they proved to be very capable run blockers and were rated amongst the nation's elite on the interior as pile movers. They return the core of that corps and center Jake Slaughter is a potential All-SEC candidate. Add in solid running back Montrell Johnson (817 rushing yards, 5.4 yards per carry) and there is a path for the Gators to smash the run, work the chains with an efficient passing game and protect their vulnerable defense. For that to happen, Florida must improve upon a 36.7% conversion rate on 3rd down and expand the offense.

Weaknesses

Young Austin Armstrong returns as defensive coordinator and he needs to see improvements quickly. The Florida defense was terrible last year, surrendering 27.6 points per game, 4.8 yards per attempt to enemy ball carriers and a fat 8.3 yards per attempt to opposing passers. The Gators gave up an unacceptable 6.4 yards per play overall and were ranked as the 75th best efficiency defense in the nation by FEI. Only Vanderbilt gave up more explosive plays than the Gators last year and that is not the conference company any team wants to keep. They lost their best pass rusher and overall defensive lineman Princely Umanmielen to Ole Miss in the portal and two cornerbacks transferred out as well. Washington veteran transfer Asa Turner will be a godsend at one safety spot and his young counterpart Jordan Castell grew up considerably last year after leading the Gators in tackles and busted coverages. Safety should be improved, possibly even quite good.

Cornerback Jason Marshall looks good in the offseason and draws all sorts of raves for his athleticism but he gave up 24.2 yards per reception and 10.8 yards every time he was targeted. His coverage opposite Devin Moore will be a first time starter as will nickel Sharif Denson. That is not necessarily a bad thing as Moore and Denson are part of a talent movement replacing poor performers, but when you watch Florida play it is not always clear what is schematic idiocy, player stupidity, or a simple lack of playmaking. The Florida pass defense surrendered a hefty 13.9 yards per completion, but somehow managed to only intercept three balls all year. A parking meter with a bucket draped on it could equal that feat. Let's see if some new faces on the back end can make more plays on the ball than five Roombas with a laundry basket duct taped on top.

Run defense must improve. The Gators were 0-5 when giving up more than 170 yards rushing despite having interior defenders in their two deep who go 325, 370 and 464. 370 would usually catch the eye, but the 464 is not a misprint. It's nose tackle Desmond Watson. I'm not saying he's fat but if he rolled over a dollar, four quarters would come out. He ties his belt with a boomerang. Florida needs more energy from their big boys inside or those three will continue to keep taking it on their six chins. Kentucky and LSU each dropped 329 yards rushing on them in blowout losses and that can't happen with Florida level talent unless some guys are opening up big boxes of quit. Florida's linebackers were equally to blame. They are not very instinctive. The health of players like pass rusher Justus Boone and linebacker Shemar James will be key to them leveling up to acceptability.

Florida's special teams coaching was a tad uneven. They were penalized for having two players wearing the same number against Utah on a punt return (the Utes scored a touchdown on that extended possession), they had less than 11 men on the field on no less than five occasions throughout the season and they lost to Arkansas when they ran out 17 men for a game-winning field goal attempt. After checking the rules, this is six more men than allowed. Never accuse this preview of not doing its homework. The Gator assistant tasked with special teams had to delete all of his social media accounts after enduring multiple threats from Gator fans. The amusing counterpoint to their lack of organization is that when Gator special teams got lined up and actually did stuff, they were ranked 6th nationally in overall efficiency. That speaks to young talent and athleticism on their coverage teams but it also helps that returning punter Jeremy Crawshaw averaged 48.9 yards per kick and finished the season as an All-American. Florida was also outstanding at kickoff return coverage. Opponents averaged only 15 yards per return and Florida had a ton of stops before the opponent could make it to the 20 yard line. The Gator roster doesn't lack athletes. They need to get them pointed in the right direction. Which is the larger story of Napier's time in Gainesville.

Speaking of speed – specifically the crystal variety — let's talk Razorbacks!

Arkansas Razorbacks
November 16 | Fayetteville, AR

Head Coach | Sam Pittman

Key Losses | QB KJ Jefferson, RB Raheim Sanders, LB Jaheim Thomas, LB Chris Paul, C Beau Limmer

Key Additions | QB Taylen Green, OT Fernando Carmona, RB Ja'Quinden Jackson

2023 Record - 4-8

The Arkansas Razorbacks would have a new coach this year if they could have afforded head coach Sam Pittman's 16 million dollar buyout. Texas A&M fans laugh (and sob) at buyouts so petty, but when your state economy is predicated on selling roadside preserves, novelty slingshots and carving rustic interior decor signs geared towards wine moms that decorate their kitchen with wisdom like Mind Your Own Biscuits And Life Will Be Gravy, it's not so easy. A state can whittle only so fast and every barter economy has its limits.

This brings to mind a joke that sums up the challenge of being an Arkansas fan. How many Arkansas football fans does it take to change a lightbulb? None. They just sit in the dark and talk about how good the lightbulb was 60 years ago.

Take last year. The light never turned on. The 4-8 Hogs had some close losses, but they made sloppy errors, committed unforced gaffes, the offense was utterly putrid and they were the Keystone Kops on special teams. As if that wasn't bad enough, the Razorbacks fired Pittman's failed coaching buddy Dan Enos and brought in Bobby Petrino as their new offensive coordinator. Yes, that Bobby Petrino. The former head coach of Arkansas who did a press conference in a neck brace covered in road rash after wrecking his motorcycle because he may or may not have been fleeing from the angry boyfriend of his former Razorback volleyball player special lady friend half his age and was fired for lying about all of it. Let's not judge the man. I think most of us have done that. Petrino is primed to be Pittman's successor and this is why the SEC is better than any soap opera ever made. Whether you prefer All My Children or All My Chitlins, the plot twists defy belief.

As for that Petrino staff hire, a little advice to you Coach Pittman: when you and your wife are having problems, don't invite Brad Pitt to live in your pool house and then go on a three week hunting trip with your buddies.

Beyond his hiring of the failed Enos and the total immolation of his offense, Pittman wasn't helped by the fact that the respected former offensive line coach was undone by the play of his primary area of expertise up front: the Razorback offensive line. They surrendered 47 sacks and the most tackles for loss of any unit in the conference. That was a major point of emphasis in the offseason and the Razorbacks attacked the portal hard after losing mainstays like running back Rocket Sanders, quarterback KJ Jefferson and linebacker Chris Paul to various rivals. Pittman must emulate West Virginia's Neal Brown who seemed all but fired before last year, but rattled off a nine win season riding the arm and legs of his dual threat quarterback and an opportunistic defense. As hard as it is to believe, there's actually a blueprint for Pittman to pull off something similar, however improbable. The problem with pulling a rabbit out of a hat in Arkansas is that someone will claim you stole their breakfast. Pittman's buyout comes down if his overall record goes below .500, so Arkansas is actually incentivized to hope that Sam either really turns it around or completely blows it. Odds are that he will try to do both.

Bottom line: Sam Pittman is 11-23 in SEC play over his first four years. He'll have Texas circled on the schedule for a JiHawg in Fayetteville, but Taylen Green will need to be exceptional behind a questionable Arkansas offensive line for them to overcome an unforgiving schedule with a job-saving season.

Strengths

The Arkansas defensive line should be very good. They're absolutely huge, averaging 6-4.5 and 297 pounds across their four man front. Immature or finesse offensive lines run the real risk of being overpowered against this bunch – Arkansas defensive linemen combined for 41 tackles for loss last year, second among all SEC peers. The best of the bunch is skyscraper defensive end Landon Jackson, a massive 6-7, 280 athlete from Texarkana who was 2nd team All-SEC last year and is fairly well regarded by NFL draft analysts. He moves well for his size and his length is a problem for QB windows even when he's blocked. He isn't an explosive pass rusher, but he's stout against the run and he can cover a lot of ground. Eric Gregory and Cameron Ball are plus run stoppers inside at a combined 645 pounds. Both likely have late round NFL futures. Edge Nico Davillier is also a big defensive end at 6-4, 270, but he's a more competent pass rusher than run defender. The backups are good and the Hogs roll deep.

Keep an eye on Albany transfer defensive end Anton Jucaj. He was a FCS All-American with 15 sacks last year. The 6-3, 270 pound athlete could easily earn a starting job and cement this unit even more. Overall, the Hogs have a Top 15 quality defensive front that plays with great physicality though not necessarily elite quickness. That means that if opposing offensive lines can hold up strength-wise, the Pig pass rush generally won't get there.

The Hogs moved on from three year starter KJ Jefferson – who will play his last year of ball at UCF for Gus Malzahn – and whether the breakup was mutual or one-sided, there's no use crying over spilled trough slop. His replacement is intriguing. The Hogs brought on talented dual threat and native Texan Taylen Green from Boise State. The 6-6 225 pound Green has an easy gliding running style that evokes You Know Who – brace yourself for the idiot color announcer babbling Vince Young comparisons – but he struggled to thrive in a poorly conceived Bronco offensive system that sought to make a spread run prototype into a pocket passer and game manager. Though the Broncos eventually fired head coach Andy Avalos for his coaching malpractice and brought back Dirk Koetter to coordinate the offense, the relationship was fractured and Green hit the market. The desperate Hogs paid up and will build out their offensive identity around Green's legs and a big arm potentially well suited to single read deep ball passing.

Potential is the key word there. Green is an extremely quirky passer. Read that as when a girl's dating profile describes herself as "quirky." It means crazy. On throws to his right 10+ yards, he completed 6 of 26 balls for 133 yards with no touchdowns. Throwing to his left 10+ yards? He was 15 of 35 for 347 yards and 3 scores. He's not accurate on either side of the hash, but he's at least dangerous throwing left. What about the middle of the field? He threw four interceptions on 16 of 38 passing. He did average 26 yards per completion on those middle throws, but you would like to see better accuracy and care for the ball.

Green is a very dangerous runner (he has three 70+ yard touchdown runs in his career) with a deceptive stride, but he has struggled to make reads and progressions in the traditional passing game and will turn it over to the other team with "What was that?" throws. Whether that's ameliorated by a more favorable QB friendly spread system remains to be seen. Whatever you think of Bobby Petrino, he is an inspired play caller.

The surrounding skill talent is adequate. Former Longhorn Ja'Quinden Jackson (6-2, 230) will start at running back and he's a good power runner with some wiggle. Andrew Armstrong is the best receiver on the team and at 6-4 he is a terrific deep threat. The Hogs love young receiving tight end Luke Hasz and he will probably be their #2 pass catcher overall. The most glaring problem with the surrounding skill talent is that it's not deep nor is any one player particularly remarkable. They really need Green and Petrino to drive this offense.

Just make sure it's not on a motorcycle.

Weaknesses

The offensive line was a disaster last year outside of returning guard Josh Braun, who is a good player. They gave up 47 sacks and the most tackles for loss in the SEC last year. Former Arkansas QB KJ Jefferson played half of his games in various states of injury, looking like a cross between Apollo Creed in Rocky IV when Drago gets him on the ropes and a pinata at Shohei Ohtani's birthday party. The other returning guard is Patrick Kutas, who gave up five sacks and a combined 41 hurries and pressures last year playing mostly tackle. Center and both tackle spots will need to be filled by transfers and Arkansas mavens must be scratching their heads wondering how a former offensive line coach at head coach can't develop homegrown starters years into his program.

The transfer group being counted on to start includes tackles Keyshawn Blackstock (Michigan State) and Fernando Carmona (San Jose St) along with center Addison Nichols (Tennessee). Carmona projects to be the best of the bunch and was a plus player for San Jose last year. Nichols couldn't break into the lineup in Knoxville and Blackstock had the same story in Lansing. It looks like the Hogs will start two viable offensive linemen and three major question marks. They can't be worse than last year and the presence of a running QB and Bobby Petrino calling plays will help them, but their ability to pass protect on predictable passing downs should be marginal at best and depth is questionable overall. If Arkansas succeeds on offense, it will be in spite of their big uglies up front.

The Hogs lost their two starting linebackers — Chris Paul and Jaheim Thomas — to Ole Miss and Wisconsin, respectively, and they were the two leading tacklers on the team. Thomas missed 14.7% of his attempted tackles, but he was an outstanding blitzer and pass rusher. Chris Paul is the bigger loss as a more traditional run defender. They'll be replaced by newcomers Brad Spence and Xavian Sorey. Sorey is a Georgia transfer who was too Sorey to play in Athens, but he's found a home in Fayetteville. Spence is a big physical sophomore from Houston, Texas with athletic ability who struggles to diagnose at times. If the linebackers are competent, the run defense will be fine given their stud defensive line, but both Sorey and Spence are unproven commodities.

The Arkansas defense was a study in bullying last year. When they faced offensive lines that their defensive line could push around, they acquitted themselves fairly well. When teams blocked them up, they gave up 34 or more points to six different opponents. Some of that scoring was set up by the putrid Enos offense, but any offense that can handle their defensive front will find the Hogs compliant. Sophomore Jaylon Braxton is their best cornerback and he has a big ceiling, but the four seniors that play with him have an uneven track record against higher tier passing offenses.

Kentucky Wildcats
November 23 | Austin, TX

Head Coach | Mark Stoops

Key Losses | RB Ray Davis, DE Keaten Wade, CB Andru Phillips

Key Additions | QB Brock Vandagriff, WR Ja'Mori Maclin, LB Jamon Dumas-Johnson, DJ Waller, RB DeaMonte Trayanum

2023 Record - 7-6

Mark Stoops probably had a few awkward conversations in Lexington this offseason. That's because Texas A&M athletic director Ross Bjork unilaterally semi-hired the UK head coach and may have even had him on a plane flying down to College Station for a press conference (internet rumors are always unimpeachable on these details), only to be thwarted by red-assed Texas A&M fans in open revolt. Eventually, the Aggie Board of Regents blocked the prospective hire. Bjork read the political winds, determined that they were largely his own flatulence and miraculously talked himself into a better job at Ohio State, proof of the inexorable rise of empty-suited athletic administrators who can dazzle college presidents with the use of the words "synergy" and "stakeholders." Texas A&M hired Duke coach Mike Elko and Stoops had to return to Lexington and do some splainin'.

"What? No, I wasn't taking the Aggie job. Was that even open? College Station is gorgeous in late November. I went to watch the leaves turn and stroll its broad boulevards. Perhaps dip into a patisserie and idle in a sidewalk cafe. Ah, Greater Bryan!"

Fortunately, it happened during basketball season and no one noticed. That's not entirely true. It was noticed, but the Wildcats have been surprisingly understanding, in part because they didn't have many cards to play. That's shocking for a state that has a history of blood feuds and harbors eternal memories of all slights against Appalachian honor, but football is firmly sport #4 in Lexington behind the basketball season, basketball recruiting season and horse racing. They won't tolerate Kentucky outright stinking on Saturdays, but their priorities are clear.

Who has the most power in any relationship? The party that cares the least. Neither one of these parties cares too much. What a great way to minimize relational drama!

Stoops has had a pretty good run in Lexington, keeping Kentucky firmly in the conference middle class after a three year initial rebuild that saw the Cats go 12-24 from 2013-2015. Since then Kentucky is 61-41 with only one losing season. That record won't blow up any skirts at Texas or Georgia, but if Kentucky beats Louisville (they're on a five game winning streak), wins their other feeble non-cons, goes 4-4 in the league with one upset of a conference headliner and only one setback against an inferior (for Wildcat fans that is Vanderbilt, Mississippi State, Arkansas, South Carolina) then Kentuckians are pleased as punch with their 8-4 record, a Music City Bowl berth and their full attention turned to March Madness.

That is the Wildcat goal every year, so that is the goal for 2024 Kentucky. Like nearly every Kentucky team under Stoops, they have outstanding players at a few spots, questions at quarterback and on the offensive line, high quality athletes all over the defense and solid if unremarkable schemes. For Kentucky, being the middle child of SEC football is just fine. They aren't always trying to rise like insecure Auburn and Texas A&M, there is no dynasty to service like Bama or Georgia, no ghosts of great teams past to haunt them like Arkansas. They enjoy the wins, flush the losses and enjoy life in a nice little college city. That's not a bad deal, is it?

Strengths

Barion Brown and Dane Key are a pair of underrated 3rd year junior wide receivers who have seen their statistical outputs hampered by mediocre Kentucky quarterbacks and ineffective passing games. Key has 79 catches and 12 touchdowns and 14.6 yards per catch over his first two years on campus and this junior year promises more of the same. He is a lanky 6-3, 195 and he's terrific at getting out of his breaks smoothly. Think possession receiver with some big play upside. Barion Brown is a skinny 6-1, 170 pound game breaker with elite quickness and deep speed. He's a legitimate 4.3 40 guy who has amassed four kickoff return touchdowns in just two years, which is tied for the all-time SEC record. Brown has 93 catches over the last two years, but Kentucky's inability to hit him deep has been a constant source of program frustration. Transfer wideout J'mori Maclin rounds out the trio. The former Missouri and North Texas athlete caught 57 balls for 1,004 yards and 11 touchdowns last year for the Mean Green and was a 2nd Team All-AAC performer. He's a terrific complement to Key and Brown. Kentucky has deeply underrated pass catching options.

Kentucky's best player is nose tackle Deone Walker. A consensus preseason All-American, Walker is 6-6, 350 and he plays like T'vondre Sweat with better conditioning and pass rush. Last season, he had 7.5 sacks, logged a ridiculous 51 pressures and was 1st team All SEC. The junior is still getting better. The future top 10 draft pick gives Kentucky's defense a great deal of latitude to scheme around him in their base defense and he's flanked by multiple huge bodies who are capable run stoppers, if negligible pass rushers. Deone is a problem that offenses had better address.

Kentucky has some very high impact players at the 2nd level of the defense. Linebacker D'Eryk Jackson is a beefy 6-1, 245 and loves contact. He led the Cats in tackles, but he is also outstanding in coverage. Last year, he had two pick offs and the 2nd highest coverage grade on the team. He's joined by Georgia transfer Jamon-Dumas Johnson. Unlike many Georgia transfers, JDJ didn't leave looking for playing time. The 6-1, 245 pound star linebacker started 24 games in Athens and was a finalist for the Butkus Award in 2022. He's a superstar, hampered last year by a foot injury. Georgia wanted to keep him, but they could not afford him. Alex Afari is their big nickel and the 6-2, 215 athlete is a plus coverage asset within the UK system. If the Kentucky linebackers stay healthy, this is a top 5 unit nationally. That may be surprising to read, but Jackson and Dumas-Johnson are the real deal.

Cornerback Maxwell Hairston had an outstanding coverage grade but he achieved it in a counterintuitive way. He's not a shutdown corner in the conventional sense as opponents completed 66% of their passes on him, but those completions averaged only 6.4 yards per attempt and less than 10 yards per reception. He concedes shallow completions, but no one can get over top of him. He eventually baits the quarterback into complacency and jumps the "automatic completion" for an interception. He had five last year, including two pick sixes. Pretty smart player. He will be joined by field cornerback DJ Waller, a very promising young man that transferred in from Michigan. Waller's transfer caught Michigan by surprise – he was expected to start on a potentially elite defense. The Cats could have a damn good corner combo.

If you are starting to think that Kentucky has the infrastructure for a potentially good defense, you are picking up what I'm putting down. They are a reliable safety and nickel and one more pass rusher away from kicking some people around.

Weaknesses

Brock Vandagriff is a mobile former 5 star quarterback from Georgia who lost highly publicized battles with Stetson Bennett and Carson Beck to be the man in Athens – no shame in that – but now he's taking his talents and 21 career pass attempts to the Bluegrass State. Just what those talents are in theory versus their translated reality on Saturdays remains to be seen. Vandagriff spent most of his career at Georgia looking like a roadie for the Allman Brothers, but the Ramblin' Man has cut his flowing locks and will be the clearcut and clean cut starter in Lexington replacing former NC State passer Devin Leary. Leary was largely a disappointment last year and the Cats are hoping that Vandagriff can unlock a strong receiver trio while adding some 3rd down conversions with his legs.

Mark Stoops is familiar with transfer QBs – they're on their third transfer starter in a row – and Vandagriff will team up with new offensive coordinator Bush Hamdan from Boise State, who, if you read the profile of Taylen Green above, may have a passer better suited to his system. Coach Hamdan has referred to his system as "caffeinated pro style" so it's possible that Hamdan is a marketing idiot. What he means is that Kentucky will play more uptempo, but in a pro style traditional offense. Any tempo at all is a big departure for Kentucky as Stoops has tended to encourage his offensive coordinators to milk the clock and shorten the game. Vandagriff has had a career marked by the P word – potential rather than performance – but this will be his offense initially. If he struggles, UK added former Rutgers starter Gavin Wimsatt. Wimsatt has plenty of data points as a starter but they're something less than stellar. He was a 47% passer last year and the Scarlet Knights encouraged him to find opportunities elsewhere.

The Kentucky safeties are decent, but risk-averse. Kentucky's pass defense has epitomized bend-but-don't-break. Opponents completed 67.6% of their balls, but those completions were limited to 10.7 yards per completion. Eventually the field constricts and offenses have to run the ball at Deone Walker and their linebackers to score. That's the theory, but it has limited success against accurate throwers with high level receivers who can create yards after the catch. Georgia lit them up by going 33 of 42 for 435 yards and 5 touchdowns. Alabama went 16 of 25 for 285 and 3 touchdowns. A schematic strength against most of their schedule should be a weakness against the Longhorns.

Kentucky's offensive line has four returning starters totaling over 130+ collective starts. That's great news. The bad news is that they didn't block very well against higher level defenses. Tackle Marques Cox is the class of the unit, but he should be. This is his 7th year of college football and he has 46 career starts. He does not make mistakes and he won't surrender sacks. Similarly, center Eli Cox is returning for his 6th year at Kentucky and he has 35 consecutive starts. He will get everyone coordinated adeptly, but he has modest physical gifts and he gave up 4 sacks last year along with a unit high 8 penalties. Guard Jager Burton (25 starts) is a poor run blocker and tackle Gerald Mincey is on his third school and has thus far defined mediocrity. This unit gives Kentucky a decent baseline and they are not soft, but high level defensive lines should handle them.

Texas A&M Aggies
November 30 | College Station, TX

2023 Record - 7-6
2024 Spring Game - 1-0
Halftime Record - Undefeated

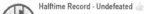

Head Coach | Mike Elko

Key Losses | Jimbo Fisher's contract offset language, DT Walter Nolen, WR Ainias Smith, LB Edgerrin Cooper

Key Additions | DE Nic Scourton, LB Solomon DeShields, OG Ar'maj Reed-Adams, CB Will Lee

The Jimbo Fisher era is over at Texas A&M. It only cost Texas A&M a 77.6 million dollar buyout and a half dozen wasted years to find out that the coach who went 5-6 in his final season at Florida State with the lowest Academic Progress Rate in all of college football and a series of player misconduct scandals might not have been a gnomic George Washington after all. Fisher's outdated offense and questionable staff hires managed two ranked seasons in six years despite top level recruiting. The Aggies were 46-27 (27-22 in SEC play) overall during his tenure. The Aggies paid him a couple of million dollars per win and they don't get rebates for the low level of difficulty for victories against UMass, New Mexico, Abilene Christian and Kent State. Tragically, Fisher did not fill any space on the empty national championship plaque that he was presented with at his introductory press conference so A&M's equestrian and meat-judging teams remain the campus standard bearers. Beyond their national title ambitions, the Aggies are still 25 years out from their last conference title. Let's walk before we run, Aggies. They are the parents who believe that their toddler's best intro to water should be an attempt to swim the English channel. Love the ambition, but let's get some floaties on, shall we?

Jimbo left twin interrelated legacies at Texas A&M: stellar recruiting rankings and impressive under-achievement. His final 7-6 team is one of the worst underachievement metrics vs. talent acquisition ever recorded, particularly given that these were Texas A&M's national composite recruiting rankings since 2020:

2019 #4 | 2020 #6 | 2021 #8 | 2022 #1

The 2022 class was considered the best ever in college football history by the consensus rankings and it raised eyebrows from SEC league mates accustomed to paying players but not on A&M's unapologetic scale and ambition. 2022 and 2023 should have been the years the talent hit with 2024 loaded for (good) bull, but A&M went 12-13 and 6-10 in SEC play during that time, including a 10 game road losing streak. A&M's 2023 winning record was abetted by home wins over UL Monroe, New Mexico and

Abilene Christian. FCS Abilene Christian had a losing record in something called the UAC conference while the G5 Lobos and Warhawks were a combined 6-18. So the Aggies weren't a very formidable 7-6 and they turned their locker room into the Real Housewives of Bryan.

So why do the Aggies have legitimate hope in 2024? First, though sizable portions of those recruiting classes are no longer in College Station, quite a few of those players are still around, just waiting to get some reasonable coaching. Second, the Aggies hired an actual football coach in former Duke headman Mike Elko, a well-respected defensive mind who already knows the program from his stint as an assistant there. Elko went 16-9 at Duke in his two years there versus the Blue Devils' 5-18 mark in two seasons prior. Third, they immediately attacked needs via the transfer portal and brought in a good combination of stars and productive role players that Elko can shape into appropriate roster fits. Fourth, Elko told the prima donnas to play ball or haul ass and he established a baseline culture.

By virtue of their national humiliation and financial idiocy, the Aggies were forced into temporary realism; briefly scrubbed of their delusion and graspingness. They actually made the unsexy hire that might actually serve them best, with necessity doing the work of reason. Without an 80 million buyout hanging over their heads, perhaps they would have tried to acquire more magic beans from passing peddlers and written Lenny Dysktra for more stock tips, but hard fiscal truths and the realization that they would not be landing Kirby Smart, Dan Campbell, Andy Reid or Bear Bryant's artificial intelligence loaded into a Simple Simon forced the Elko hire and a difficult embrace of reality. That was probably the best possible result. Elko is a pragmatist and you can expect A&M to do the simple things first in order to raise the floor of the program.

Texas A&M has a compliant league schedule. They host Texas, Missouri and LSU and their worst road games are at Florida and Auburn. No Georgia, no Bama, no Ole Miss, no Oklahoma, no Tennessee. Mike Elko is well positioned to have a good first year in College Station if he can change the culture there from counting their chickens before they hatch to actually developing their roosters.

Strengths

The Aggie defensive line is very good and Purdue transfer Nic Scourton is a big reason why. The Bryan native's value proposition is simple: he's 6-4, 280, looks even bigger than that, and moves like he's 250. You can't run at him either. A&M has good personnel around him. Shemar Turner and Albert Regis are stout inside and transfer Cashius Howell from Bowling Green had 9.5 sacks last year and is a good option when they want to go with quickness on the edge opposite Scourton. When they want to go with size, they will turn to 6-6, 285 pound Shemar Stewart. The Aggies promise to have a stout front against the run and they should be able to mount a very reasonable pass rush. Depth is solid with sophomore DJ Hicks – a former five star – hunting for snaps inside. Texas A&M is probably starting three NFL guys up front with some big talent loading the depth chart behind them and that's always a nice foundation to build the larger defense around.

Quarterback Conner Weigman played as a true freshman and impressed only to see last year's strong start truncated by injury. The 3rd year QB has tantalized at times in limited action (his 8:1 TD/INT ratio isn't shabby either) and NFL scouts love his arm, easy release, running ability and ability to throw accurately on the move. If he has a strong year, he might be gone. Still, we don't have many data points to judge him. Over his career Weigman is 155 of 251 for 1851 yards with 16 tds and 2 interceptions and a 61.8% completion rate. By contrast, two year Texas starter Quinn Ewers already has 690 college attempts under his belt. Weigman appears to be good, but the sample size for that opinion is questionable at best.

Weigman throws very catchable balls with zip, which is a rare combination. He also runs well enough to punish defenses that play man-to-man or ignore containment in their pass rush. While Weigman has a live arm and the ability to deliver accurately while on the move, he tends to sail the ball outside of the hashes and he has some bad back foot throwing habits when under pressure. It's important to consider that despite his undeserved guru reputation, Jimbo Fisher was a terrible offensive coordinator and QB coach who over-coached mechanics and had an offense that resembled a Rube Goldberg Machine. Even simple tasks required arduous complexity. Weigman will progress simply by playing in a more reasonable college system. With a healthy 2024, some NFL draftniks believe that he is fully capable of being a 1st round NFL draft pick. That fact speaks to his ability, the NFL's desperation for QBs and a softer 2025 class in equal measure.

Aggie running backs Jamari Daniels and Le'Veon Moss are quality ball carriers who should see their production increase with a better QB, a less porous OL and better overall coaching. Rueben Foster provides an intriguing big play component, but he averaged only 3.8 yards per carry last year.

Is the Aggie linebacker corps a strength or weakness? Hard to tell yet. They lost Edgerrin Cooper to the NFL, a fantastic player who was by far the best and most consistent performer on the roster, but they brought back undersized Taurean York who showed out well as a run defender and team leader. York is quick and exhibits good play strength despite his lack of size. They also added Pittsburgh linebacker Solomon Deshields who was solid for the Panthers last year. Deshields doesn't miss tackles and he can run. They also added the aptly named Scooby Williams from Florida. Scooby solves mysteries. Mysteries like how can a guy so athletic make so few plays? Zoinks. He missed 22% of his attempted tackles and in coverage he gave up a 81% completion rate.

Weaknesses

Texas A&M has a clear road for progress on both the offensive line and defensive backfield and if they do manage to traverse both successfully, there's little reason to consider either group a weakness, but until those big question marks are addressed, featuring them as strengths makes little sense.

The Aggies will rely heavily on transfers in the secondary to upgrade a unit that lacked efficiency and got hit hard by the passing games of Miami, Ole Miss, Alabama and Oklahoma State last season. They will also start a couple of players that didn't care much for tackling and Elko won't tolerate that in a system built around limiting big gains and hitting underneath receivers hard to limit yards after catch. If you include the nickel, the Aggie two deep will feature 6 out of 10 transfers with at least two of them counted on to be starters. Many of them are experienced players from lower level football, so we'll find out quickly what kind of eye Elko has for defensive backs and their skill transfer. The expectation is that he has a pretty good one, but he aimed for reliable over potential on some of his takes.

Returning starting nickel Bryce Anderson is good in coverage, but he is a somewhat unreliable tackler who does not always set the edge on outside zone. He missed 25% of his tackle attempts and opponents completed 31 of 36 balls targeted directly at him, albeit for negligible yardage at 9 yards per completion. He needs better coaching because the ability is there. One safety will be big Central Michigan transfer Trey Jones. Jones is 215 pounds, he has started a lot of games and is a physical tackler but he didn't earn All-MAC plaudits and his ability to level up to the SEC is questionable from an athletic standpoint. Can he turn and run with Texas' #3 receiver if he has to? The other safety is 2nd year sophomore Dalton Brooks. The Aggies love his raw ability, but he has little game experience, logging only 170 snaps last year.

At cornerback, the Aggies have real potential, but they need their transfers to hit in order to upgrade a pass defense that will see at least three or four high level passing attacks this year. Three of the four on the two deep are new to Aggieland. One coverage spot belongs to holdover Tyreek Chappell (29 career starts in maroon and white) and he graded out pretty well last year despite getting lit up by the Miami Hurricanes for three touchdowns early in the season. After that game, he only surrendered one touchdown the entire rest of the year. He is an abysmal tackler. He whiffed or got run through on 23% of his tackle attempts last year.

Former UAB starting cornerback B.J. Mayes was very solid for the Blazers last year, but they were a 4-8 AAC team and he may find facing Texas and Missouri wide receivers different from taking on Temple and North Carolina A&T. The Aggies probably got a big bump with the addition of former Kansas State cornerback Will Lee. The long 6-3, 190 corner has great wingspan and he is an excellent off man and zone defender. Lee graded out well for the Wildcats last year but he did get hit over the top for big gains against Missouri, UCF and Baylor. Peeking into the backfield is the main culprit. He spent some time in the doghouse in Manhattan, but the reasons are unclear. The final corner piece is Alabama transfer Dezz Ricks. A former five star, Ricks has big time potential, but he didn't log much work at Bama with two high NFL draft picks ahead of him.

The A&M offensive line has some quality players, but they have not had particularly good coaching and several played out of position last year. The unit will shuffle the deck chairs and hope that it's a Carnival cruise and not the Titanic. 6-7 315 pound left tackle Trey Zuhn is the best player on the unit and he should have a strong senior campaign. Zuhn is a quality run and pass blocker with NFL potential. They are counting on big Reuben Fatheree to lock down right tackle. The 6-8 blocker missed most of last year with injuries but logged almost 1,400 snaps in 2021 and 2022. He is a pretty talented player and a healthy Fatheree would give A&M upper half of the league bookend tackles.

The interior OL could get messy if new A&M OL coach Adam Cushing can't figure out his best combos and get more consistent run blocking. Mark Nabou started at guard last year and played average ball. He may have to move to center if Utah transfer Kolinu'u Faaiu does not impress. Nabou is a huge 325+ and can generate power, but he may be too slow-footed leaking on to 2nd level defenders. Freshman Chase Bisontis was pressed into emergency action early at tackle and he was a miserable pass protector. He gave up 4 sacks and 27 hits or hurries. He will move to guard and should be more effective there. Kansas transfer Ar'maj Reed-Adams is likely the other guard. He's an average player with a lot of experience under his belt. The best upside for the A&M offensive line is pretty good. The worst possible downside is that players don't take to their new spots and A&M has another mess on its hands.

A&M has a solid wide receiver room, but right now they profile as a bunch of #2 and #3 receivers with no single athlete outside who puts the fear of God into defenses. They also have little variation in body type. Noah Thomas, Moose Muhammad and Jahdae Walker should be fine in aggregate and size won't be a problem – the three average 6-4, 205 pounds – so they should win more than their share of jump balls and contested catches. Can any of them consistently win vertically or after the catch? Can any of them shake open in a tight space? That remains to be seen.

THE REST OF THE SEC

Texas doesn't play these teams, but their games with Texas opponents have conference and national implications. Several of them have relatively favorable schedules and that could certainly impact teams like Texas, Georgia and Alabama with respect to a SEC title game berth. Learn a little about the seven SEC teams that are not on the Texas schedule.

OLE MISS

There's a lot to like about Ole Miss this year and it's more than just tailgating, flirting with Southern belles and Lane Kiffin's masterful trolling on Twitter. The Rebels return star senior QB Jaxson Dart, a strong group of pass catchers led by Tre Harris, Jordan Watkins and tight end Caden Prieskorn and the best transfer portal class in America. Ole Miss has always had legitimate skill players on offense, but this portal class sought to address all of the other areas where they come up short against the big boys: the line of scrimmage and defense. This outstanding haul may have finally given them the infrastructure that they need to be effective against the league's juggernauts.

Yes, they won a school record 11 games last year, including a nice win over Penn State in the Peach Bowl, but Georgia blew them out 52-17 in a game that was absolutely non-competitive and Alabama dominated the Rebel offense 24-10. Even narrow wins over Texas A&M and LSU turned into perilous shootouts. Ole Miss couldn't get stops against real offenses and against the league's best defenses offensive line deficits came to the fore and Kiffin's high flying offense was shut down. Ole Miss needed more weapons, more infrastructure, more speed and more big, angry football players who don't take kindly to being pushed around. So they went out and bought them.

The parallels to last year's mercenary Florida State team are clear. The Rebels added to the offensive skill mix with the addition of South Carolina WR Juice Wells and four running backs, but more importantly they upgraded the offensive line with Washington transfers Nate Kalepo and Julius Buelow and North Carolina's Diego Pounds. The real overhaul came on defense though. They enticed Texas A&M defensive tackle Walter Nolen, Florida edge Princely Umanmielen, Arkansas backer Chris Paul and three new secondary starters from Alabama and Houston. Added to a decent homegrown core of returnees, Ole Miss has a real chance to field a high level offense that may not fold against dominant defensive lines and a defense that can do some bullying of its own.

The schedule works out quite well. The Rebels' four non-conference opponents are Georgia Southern, Furman, Middle Tennessee and Wake Forest. Way to really push yourselves there, guys. In SEC play, they also avoid Alabama, Texas and Missouri as well as potential upstarts Tennessee and Texas A&M. They do play Georgia, but in Oxford. LSU and Oklahoma could be good, but right now Ole Miss would be favored in both contests. Their opportunity is a unique confluence between a favorable SEC draw, a feeble non-conference schedule and their best balance of talent at all positions in some time. Expect Lane Kiffin to make some hay while the sun shines, but remain skeptical that they can compete at the highest levels until they prove it.

ALABAMA

The GOAT Nick Saban is gone after 17 years and six national titles in Tuscaloosa. You can find numerous essays extolling his virtues and celebrating his legacy but this quick and dirty profile has no time for it. In summary: Hey, good job, Nick.

Alabama can't duplicate what Saban did and they needed to hire the best replacement they could find as quickly as possible to stem a portal exodus. So Alabama hired former Washington head coach Kalen DeBoer. Smart move. DeBoer was 25-3 at Washington over the last two years, including a national title game appearance and he boasts a 2-0 record against Texas. He has a 104-12 record as a head coach overall at multiple programs at multiple levels of football. DeBoer is a brilliant offensive mind and an absolute winner. Is he a good fit at Alabama? Can he recruit at the highest levels? – much of his Washington team was inherited from Chris Petersen. Can he adapt culturally? That remains to be seen, but our task is to focus on 2024 Alabama.

DeBoer will be good for Jalen Milroe – he has a history utilizing dual threat QBs at stops prior to Washington (Michael Penix isn't the only QB the man has ever coached) and Milroe throws the kind of catchable deep ball that DeBoer covets in his pupils. Jalen also protects the ball (very few turnover worthy throws once he got past his difficulties vs. Texas, he's not a fumbler when sacked) and his 500+ scramble yards are hidden chain movers and a godsend to a college offense. Milroe will play behind a strong offensive line that has worked through last year's growing pains at tackle and come out the other end as a force to be reckoned with. If the young tackles continue to blossom as hoped, this unit could grow into the nation's best.

Wide receiver is below typical Alabama standards and DeBoer brought in former Husky Germie Bernard to help buffer an inexperienced position group and complement holdovers Kobe Prentice and Kendrick Law. The Tide could really use one more difference maker outside and we will see if that athlete is hidden in plain sight somewhere on the roster. A running back by committee will include Jam Miller and Justice Haynes with some promising young freshman talent. Alabama will score points, but the offense may be more deliberate and considered than the highlight reel scoreboard assaults that took place in Seattle. Milroe is far from a finished product, but he can take over a game and his pure physical strength makes him difficult to wear down.

The Tide defense looks fairly strong, but they need to redo the secondary. The addition of excellent Michigan transfer Keon Sabb was a pleasant surprise to help make up for the departure of safety Caleb Downs. Cornerback Domani Brown transferred in from USC and he should be decent. Right now the other corner looks like it will be manned by true freshman 5 star Zabien Brown. Early word on Brown is that he is a superstar, but let's check back once he takes some live bullets from Missouri's Luther Burden or stops Tennessee's vertical game. The underappreciated Malachi Moore will be strong at the other safety spot. Linebacker and the defensive front are good to go, but they lack elite star power and it is not clear who will get after the passer for them. This should be a good, not great unit overall. They will face several of the SEC's best offenses, so it's important that they find their sea legs quickly or risk losing some shootouts.

If almost any other head coach had taken over after Nick Saban, predicting Alabama to have a 8-4 record would be fairly easy given their challenging SEC schedule and various vultures raiding their talent with NIL promises, but DeBoer does not give games away and the Tide have enough on the offensive line, at running back and quarterback to bully and control softer SEC defenses like LSU, Missouri and Tennessee. The Tide plays those three teams consecutively starting in late October. Throw in hosting Georgia in Tuscaloosa and a road trip to Norman and Alabama might not weather the storm to earn a SEC title game shot, but they can play spoiler in interesting ways that could very well benefit the Longhorns.

 # AUBURN

Auburn fans endured a miserable 6-7 season under 1st year head coach Hugh Freeze that saw them lose on their home field to New Mexico St, get blown out in their bowl in a no-show performance to an ACC scrub and had their hearts ripped out in Jordan-Hare by Alabama (ahem...now Texas) receiver Isaiah Bond on a 4th and 31 miracle. Brutal year. Nearly a brutal decade.

Things haven't been so great on The Plains of late. Auburn's record since 2020? 23-26. Including a 14-20 record in SEC play. They have only won double digit games three times since 2007. What to do in the face of all of this negative misery? Rally around NIL funding and land a top 10 recruiting class! Welcome to the SEC, where the dream never dies! War Damn Eagle, y'all!

War Eagle fans were certainly critical of quarterback Payton Thorne last season, often for good reason, but they too often fail to mention that the Tigers had the worst receiving corps in the SEC and a spotty offensive line that surrendered 31 sacks and a lot of hits on the quarterback. As absurd as this is to write, Freeze may have overachieved offensively with the poor cards he was dealt. Running a functional SEC offense without a single wide receiver on the roster who would make the current Longhorn two deep is no easy task. They were dealt some new cards this offseason when Auburn considerably upgraded their wide receiver room with 5 star superstar freshman Cam Coleman (who will start from Day 1) and some solid portal additions like Robert Lewis and KeAndre Lambert-Smith. FIU transfer TE Rivaldo Fairweather caught 38 balls last year and he could be a reception monster in the Freeze play action offense.

Payton Thorne revealed himself as a very capable runner (515 yards rushing last year) and if his downfield play action passing can improve with much better options to throw to, it should also improve the efficiency of outstanding running back Jarquez Hunter. Hunter is a great blend of vision, power and slipperiness and he forces a missed tackle on a third of his carries. He is a nuanced runner and a pleasure to watch. The Auburn offensive line remains a work in progress, but they can run block and Freeze is pretty solid at minimizing deficits and finding a defense's weak spot in their run fits.

Defensively, Auburn is always going to compete and have its share of freaks but the run defense needs to improve dramatically so that they can get teams into 3rd and long and unleash a pretty good group of pass rushers and blitzers like Eugene Asante and Jalen McLeod. Former Texas safety Jerrin Thompson will lock down the back end at one safety spot. Whatever his faults, he is a veteran upgrade for them. Hiring DJ Durkin as defensive coordinator is an interesting move and he seems to enjoy a better reputation among fellow coaches than college football fans. A great deal of their season upside rests on beating Oklahoma and Texas A&M at home and Hugh Freeze knows that. That is an ambition that Texas fans can certainly get behind. Auburn will be somewhat improved and Freeze has the coaching cajones to adopt asymmetrical strategies to win games, but any talk of them as a conference dark horse is hot take nonsense.

 # LOUISIANA STATE

The Tigers lost Heisman Trophy winner Jayden Daniels and a pair of 1st round NFL draft pick wide receivers from a fantastic offense. That would usually be a major concern for any program, but LSU's offense will decline from excellent to just good. They return the best pair of offensive tackles in the game, a strong interior set of blockers and cannon-armed QB Garrett Nussmeier, who has been patiently waiting for his moment. He threw for 395 yards in LSU's bowl win over Wisconsin and he should be very effective. He is a statue in the pocket, but LSU protects well enough to keep pigeons from soiling him. Wideout Kyren Lacy returns and elite Liberty deep threat CJ Daniels and under-the-radar stud Mississippi State transfer Zavon Thomas join him along with some other solid receiver talent already on the roster. LSU will throw the ball around just fine, as they evidenced in their Spring Game.

Don't worry about them on offense. Running back doesn't appear to be as talented as usual with the departure of Logan Diggs, but the real concern for the Tigers is on defense.

LSU struggled to stop the run last year, giving up an explosive run on 18% of all runs defended. When they played teams that could throw, they also struggled to shut down the pass, finishing 92nd in team coverage and ranked 88th in explosives allowed according to Pro Football Focus. They added Missouri defensive coordinator Blake Baker this offseason and he will work to optimize a surprisingly mediocre core of upperclassmen (outside of LB Harold Perkins) while infusing better, but inexperienced talent at some key spots like cornerback. It is unclear how LSU is so bereft of defensive talent. They are the default school for all Louisiana athletes, East Texas talent is just a short drive away, the football culture is a blast, there are no pesky academics to be bothered with and they are convenient to talent goldmines like Georgia and Florida. LSU finished ranked 102nd in the country by advanced statistics FEI metrics in overall defense and frankly watching them play felt worse than that.

There is some indication that this LSU defense will at least be better at rushing the passer and Blake Baker will iron out some shoddy fundamentals, so it is not unreasonable to believe that even if LSU descends from the best offense in college football a Top 20 unit, the defense could raise its game from the Top 100 to the Top 60. That should be enough for a successful year, but an early season matchup with USC looms large in addition to hosting Alabama and Ole Miss.

T TENNESSEE

Former Sooner QB and Vol head coach Josh Heupel has done a terrific job reviving Tennessee's long defunct football program to national relevance. He's 27-13 over his first three years after taking over a program that had gone 20-27 in the four years prior. Once a national power, Tennessee has not consistently won double digit games since the 1990s. 2023's Top 20 finish meant back-to-back ranked seasons, something that the Vols hadn't accomplished since 2005. Now they have a potentially elite passer in young Nico Iamaleava and the future looks bright. The 6'6" passer has a cannon arm and was seemingly designed in a lab to run Josh Heupel's deep passing attack. That Nico can also run is an added bonus that the Vols will use advisedly. To spice up their passing game they added underrated Tulane wide receiver Chris Braswell and offensive tackle Lance Heard. Braswell will join Bru McCoy and Squirrel White in what should be a relatively strong wide receiver room. RB Dylan Sampson takes over the reins in the backfield and the 5-10, 195 pounder can scoot. The offensive line is experienced, but not overly talented so expect Nico to run around a bit before he launches his 65 yard javelins.

Tennessee will be pretty good. Not good enough to win the league unless Nico is some sort of orange day-glo demigod, but good enough to beat any team that they play. A shaky defense – other than outstanding future NFL 1st round edge James Pearce Jr. – means that they will be vulnerable to anyone that isn't a conference cellar dweller. The Vols will be highly entertaining appointment viewing and they should be involved in at least a half dozen shootouts this season.

 # MISSOURI

Eliah Drinkwitz turned it around last year with an 11-2 season and a bowl game victory over Ohio State after an inauspicious first three years stumbling about that saw the Tigers go 17-19 under his leadership. The Tigers look well positioned to have another successful year on the strength of a favorable schedule and an extremely good offense that will try to compensate for what should be a very average defense. The schedule is incredibly soft and if they can win at Texas A&M in early October, they will very likely be 6-0 rolling into a stretch of Auburn, Alabama, Oklahoma, with their final three games against Mississippi State, Arkansas and South Carolina. That is as soft as it gets in the SEC and it could land the 5th or 6th best team in the league a SEC title game shot.

The offense is loaded with experience and sheer competence across the board. QB Brady Cook represents the highest level of athletic game manager attainable. That's praise, not an insult. Wide receivers Luther Burden (86 catches, 1212 yards) and Theo Wease (49 catches, 682 yards) are also back. Burden is an absolute stud and the Tigers do a nice job of scheming him open. They will miss outstanding running back Cody Schrader immensely (1627 rushing yards, 22 touchdowns) but Drinkwitz managed to add Marcus Carroll (1350 yards rushing at Georgia State) and Nate Noel from Appalachian State to replace him. Wonderful additions. Carroll is a no-nonsense chain mover and the dexterous Noel has over 3,000 career rushing yards and had 651 rushing yards in his first five games of 2023 before succumbing to an ankle injury. The Mizzou offensive line is quality but thin. They were one of the most efficient pass protection units in college football last year and they are credible run blockers. The offense looks top notch.

So what's not to love? The defense. Missouri had five defenders drafted, including both starting cornerbacks, a safety, their best linebacker and 1st round defensive end Darius Robinson. Worse, they lost defensive coordinator Blake Baker to LSU, an innovative coach that may have seen the writing on the wall (and on LSU's check) with respect to Mizzou's remaining defensive depth chart. Missouri is not Georgia. They can't just shrug off losing five players to the NFL and carry on. They worked feverishly to add bodies in the portal and some of them – like Pitt cornerback Toriano Pride – can play, but at too many other spots they are replacing NFL players with basic college starters. There's a big difference between the two and the Missouri faithful are going to find out quickly what that difference is. Missouri's experience and offensive talent should drag them first across the finish line on most Saturdays, even if opponents score on them with a little too much ease.

If you noticed a recurring theme after reading the Missouri, Tennessee and LSU write-ups of high level offenses paired with questionable defenses, then you are reading not only for pleasure but retention and comprehension. These three teams represent interesting X factors and should be general agents of chaos – capable of upsetting the conference elite, but also quite vulnerable to teams like Kentucky, Florida or Arkansas if they don't bring their A-games.

SOUTH CAROLINA

Since Steve Spurrier left in 2015, South Carolina is 27-39 in conference play. That's a 41% winning percentage achieved in the more favorable SEC East. The dissolution of conference divisions does the Gamecocks no favors and head coach Shane Beamer should consider six regular season wins a success. Three laughable non-cons and Vanderbilt will get them to four wins and then they have to figure out a way to upset some good football teams. That will take some doing as South Carolina will start a typically subpar offensive line (41 sacks surrendered last year, dead last in rushing offense) with new quarterback redshirt freshman LaNorris Sellers. The Gamecocks appear to have bottom of the barrel wide receivers and running back Rocket Sanders – a very talented transfer from Arkansas – is made of glass. Expect North Texas transfer Oscar Adaway to play a lot in his stead. Back to QB. Sellers is a dynamic runner and huge athlete (4.6 40 at 240 pounds) who is a bit of a Palmetto State schoolboy legend, but he is an inconsistent thrower and has little game experience. That all written, South Carolina fans and players rave about his playmaking. Is this SEC doormat delusion praying for their chosen one? Of course! Stranger things have happened and he wouldn't be the first QB to come out of obscurity and put a team on his back, but there's a lot of wishcasting involved in that exercise.

The South Carolina defense has linebackers and defensive tackles almost at the conference elite tier level, but they lack edges, enough quality defensive backs and depth. That's why opponents converted nearly 45% of their money-downs against the Gamecocks last year. South Carolina was dead last in the conference in sacks and they are likely to start a true freshman five star recruit at one edge spot in an attempt to remedy that. The Gamecocks also struggle with penalties, suffering over seven per game on average. They should be able to bully poor offenses, but until proven otherwise, higher level units will spread them out and light them up. The Cocks have a wonderful and loyal fanbase, but unless Sellers is a force of nature, their pathway to a solid season is long, tenuous and narrow.

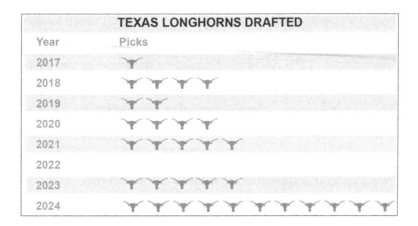

TEXAS LONGHORNS DRAFTED	
Year	Picks
2017	Y
2018	Y Y Y Y
2019	Y Y
2020	Y Y Y Y
2021	Y Y Y Y Y
2022	
2023	Y Y Y Y Y
2024	Y Y Y Y Y Y Y Y Y Y Y

The 2024 NFL Draft saw 11 Longhorns selected, good for 2nd place overall (behind national champion Michigan) and Texas' first double digit performance in the modern draft era. With 5 Longhorn players going in the first 52 players selected, it's not only the best performance from the Horns since the draft went to seven rounds three decades ago, but also arguably the best overall performance in school history.

Why?

The amazing 1984 Horns draft class had 17 athletes drafted – which broke a 38 year record held by Notre Dame – but 7 of those picks happened after Round 7. They remain the best class in Texas history by pure volume, but only 10 of them would have been drafted in the modern format.

Eight of the eleven Longhorn draftees were program homegrown and three were transfers. That's probably the mix Texas should aspire to going forward.

2024 SEC PREDICTIONS

Georgia	7-1
Texas	7-1
Alabama	6-2
Missouri	6-2
Ole Miss	6-2
Tennessee	5-3
Texas A&M	5-3
Oklahoma	4-4
LSU	4-4
Kentucky	3-5
Florida	3-5
Auburn	3-5
Arkansas	2-6
South Carolina	2-6
Mississippi State	1-7
Vanderbilt	0-8

From a pure power rating perspective Georgia profiles as the best team in the league. A step behind them, Texas. Ole Miss and Alabama are right there, each possessing a conference title game upside. Missouri, Texas A&M, Tennessee, LSU and Oklahoma are all within a similar tranche. Dangerous, but with large questions that even their coaches don't yet know the answers. Predicting record differential between those five is predicated more on schedule and match-ups than wide differences in quality, but every one of them has an X factor that could elevate them. Kentucky, Florida and Auburn represent the league's middle class. Each is fully capable of beating any team in the league on any given Saturday, but are also vulnerable to the basement dwellers on a bad day. The bottom four are Arkansas, South Carolina, Vanderbilt and Mississippi State. If Arkansas and South Carolina defy expectation, the season postscript will be about their dual threat quarterbacks surprising and delighting. Vanderbilt and Mississippi State just don't have the hosses.

SEC RECRUITING & TALENT

Texas will face better talent every week than what they faced in the Big 12. How much better? Recruiting rankings tell an interesting story. Though the portal will continue to be a means of building out rosters, cherry picking stars and filling needs, traditional recruiting remains the lifeblood of nearly every major football program, particularly in building out vital trench infrastructure. In modern college football free agency, high school recruiting is also important because it allows teams "first pass" at whether to retain talent or draw more cards from the deck.

By the final 2024 consensus recruiting rankings, seven SEC schools finished in the Top 10. That's Georgia, Alabama, Texas, LSU, Auburn, Oklahoma and Florida. Yes, the 7th best recruiting class in the SEC was a Top 10 national class. More notable is that a 6-7 Auburn team that was blown out at home by New Mexico State and pummeled in their bowl game by Maryland still signed an elite class by virtue of NIL, alumni focus and recruiting doggedness. Hugh Freeze famously didn't review Auburn's bowl game plan because he was too busy recruiting. That's understandably irritating to Auburn fans, but nearly defensible in the big picture if the goal is to get Auburn back to SEC title contention. They need players. No one will remember how they fared in a fifth rate bowl game.

Want a further illustration of madness? Florida was a disappointing 5-7 and lost five in a row to end the year. Many Gator fans are fairly certain that they will fire Billy Napier, who is 10-14 as the head coach. They still signed a Top 10 class, including a potential superstar QB of the future.

The point is that in the SEC, the teams doing well continue to prosper, while the teams who are failing recruit even harder and feverishly mobilize resources to get back to where they belong. Or where they think they belong. Part of the SEC's charm is that a dozen different fan bases feel that their team can legitimately win the national championship. There is no equivalent to that anywhere. Even when they despise their coach and are beaten down by a decade of pain, no one throws up their hands and quits. No one accepts their fate as a league doormat, save perhaps Vandy and even they thrash around from time to time. This distinguishes the SEC uniquely from all other conferences. There is a vitality curve unmatched in its ambition and cruelty.

More broadly, 13 of the Top 25 rated 2024 consensus recruiting classes belonged to SEC schools. The remainder of SEC representation in that Top 25 was rounded out by Tennessee, Texas A&M, Ole Miss, South Carolina and Kentucky. Texas A&M still landed a #17 class while replacing their coach after a season of turmoil, 5-7 South Carolina still finished 20th despite no historical indication that they'll ever be anything but a SEC whipping boy and Kentucky's head coach was allegedly on a plane to take the Aggie job before being Bjorked and still managed to ink a Top 25 group.

By the way, Arkansas (4-8 in 2023, Pittman not fired due to a money crunch) and Mississippi State (5-7, lost Leach, fired disastrous one year replacement, hastily hired Lebby) finished 26th and 28th. So that's 15 SEC schools represented in the final 2024 Top 28 recruiting rankings despite major headwinds of some variety at nearly half of the schools represented. **When SEC schools fail, they try harder.**

What about our old stomping grounds? The best 2024 Big 12 recruiting class – Texas Tech – finished 23rd in the country. That would have been good for 13th in the SEC. Arkansas, which finished 2nd to last in SEC recruiting rankings, would have finished 2nd overall in the Big 12.

2024 LONGHORN RECRUITING CLASS EVALUATION

Brought to you by special guest contributor Eric Nahlin. If you're a recruiting enthusiast and you're not a member of Inside Texas, you're missing out. Eric's encyclopedic knowledge and information networks are second to none.

Recruiting cycles often evolve into a central theme.

In the 2023 class, it was eye-opening that 12 Texas signees won at least one state championship in high school.

On Signing Day for that class, Steve Sarkisian said, "We've assembled a bunch of winners. I think we've got a culture here that is starting to understand the importance of why we're here — to win — and the idea of being competitive in everything we do. Now, we're bringing in another influx of players that is driven and focused. My idea is that you surround yourself with like-minded people that are winners, that should raise the level of all of us to perform to a point that we're about winning. That's what we're here to do."

Another way to measure whether a player is driven and focused is if he's an early enrollee. That doesn't apply to everyone, of course, there are always outliers, but it is a good indication of where a player's priorities lie.

The championship-laden 2023 class had 14 early enrollees. That was a lot. The 2024 class followed up with 18! That's become the central theme for that class.

What this means is we're also no longer just operating off network rankings or potentially misleading high school evaluations. Though we'll supply some ranking information, given so many players have been on campus for over six months, that information has outlived much of its usefulness. With so many early enrollees I'll be writing this section with the benefit of information learned from winter conditioning, spring football, and summer workouts and 7 on 7.

The most current, relevant information is the spirit of this annual, after all.

Colin Simmons, Edge, Duncanville (Texas)
On3 Industry Ranking: 98.36, 5-star, No. 15 in the nation

The recruitment: Texas defeated LSU in a come-from-behind nail-biter.

The player: The Vitruvian Man at Buck. Exceptionally well-balanced athlete with quickness, power, and motor. Has requisite athleticism to drop into coverage or rush from different angles.

The skinny: Simmons had a solid spring practice bloc but the addition of portal transfer Trey Moore will steal some snaps. Still, expect Simmons to carve out a role similar to Anthony Hill in the early going of 2023.

Brandon Baker, OT, Santa Ana (Calif) Mater Dei
On3 IR: 96.92, 4-star, No. 34

The recruitment: Texas beat Oregon and Ohio State for the near five-star tackle.

The player: Ever heard of Kelvin Banks? Baker is very similar as a player, though perhaps not quite as ready-made. He could play right tackle or left tackle eventually.

The skinny: In previous years Baker would be forced to start but Kyle Flood's room is mature and experienced. Baker arrived focused and earned respect for his work ethic. He still has some physical maturing to do but he has future star written all over him. He'll be a multi-year starter and live up to the hype.

Kobe Black, CB, Waco (Texas) Connally
On3 IR: 96.70, 4-star, No. 37

The recruitment: Texas beat A&M, LSU, and Oklahoma State where his brother plays.

The player: Black is a plus-sized boundary corner, somewhat similar to Ryan Watts. As he continues to fill out he could become a star (nickel) or perhaps even safety. I'm not ruling out cornerback, however, as moving about the football field comes easy to him.

The skinny: Most remember Ryan Wingo getting the best of him in the spring game but Wingo will do that to more seasoned corners this year. Black isn't ready to start but that's fine, he's not needed at this time.

Ryan Wingo, WR, St. Louis (Mo) St. Louis University
On3 IR: 96.70, 4-star, No. 38

The recruitment: Texas walked down Tennessee, Michigan, and Missouri before having to hold off Missouri at the last minute.

The player: He should have been a five-star. He is big, fast (10.55 100m), and a good route runner. Ball skills appear to be in place as well.

The skinny: Everyone raves about his work ethic and humble demeanor. Having met about 40 of his family members after the spring game I can assure you this is a player and family to root for. I'm not sure any player on the entire roster gained more praise during spring. Despite Sarkisian preferring a short rotation at receiver, Wingo will play this year. Future Top 15 pick.

Xavier Filsaime, S, McKinney (Texas)
On3 IR: 96.67, 4-star, No. 41

The recruitment: Texas offered the Florida commit very late in the process but the more UF faltered the more opportunity knocked. He was one of two Florida flips.

The player: Rangy, speedy safety who should excel in the coverage aspects of the position. He'll need to add some weight in order to bring physicality to bear.

The skinny: A priority of the staff was to increase speed at safety. That's the first and foremost box Filsaime checks. He's still a little raw as a player and needs some time in the weight room but he has speed you can't teach. Safety is not an easy position to learn. Even the great ones, like Caleb Downs, get beat deep early in their career. Fortunately for Texas, Filsaime won't be rushed to the field this year but he could be a natural replacement for Andrew Mukuba in 2025.

Jerrick Gibson, RB, Bradenton (Fla) IMG Academy
On3 IR: 93.90, 4-star, No. 117

The recruitment: Gibson was a one-time Florida commit but once Tashard Choice got his hooks in him, Florida, Georgia, Miami, and Tennessee didn't have a chance.

The player: A bowling ball with great downhill velocity and enough agility that he's not just a straight-line runner. He's a very powerful young man with good speed.

The skinny: Gibson had a good spring. His position is loaded but he might be able to carve out an early role on special teams. His future is bright, he just has some studs ahead of him on the assembly line.

Wardell Mack, CB, Marrero (La) John Ehret
On3 IR: 93.12, 4-star, No. 143

The recruitment: Mack was the other defensive back Texas flipped from Florida. Terry Joseph's patient recruiting approach paid off yet again.

The player: Long-armed and physical, Mack also has the movement skills to play field corner. Over time, however, he could turn into a Star. There's an element of physicality to his game.

The skinny: Like Black, he had a solid spring but isn't quite ready for primetime. Texas has a handful of experienced cornerback options ahead of him. Big upside, though.

Zina Umeozulu, Edge, Allen (Texas)
On3 IR: 92.83, 4-star, No. 161

The recruitment: Similar to his brother Neto, Zina took his time and considered Oklahoma and A&M.

The player: He has some filling out to do but with a thick neck and long limbs that's not the least bit concerning. Jack, the strong-side Edge, is not the easiest position to find quality prospects but Umeozulu is tailor-made for it.

The skinny: He'll likely get to redshirt this season given seasoned players in front of him like Barryn Sorrell, Ethan Burke, and Justice Finkley. There's plenty of excitement around his future.

Aaron Butler, WR, Calabasas (Calif)
On3 IR: 91.74, 4-star, No. 213

The recruitment: Butler was offered incredibly late in the process but because Steve Sarkisian and Chris Jackson had relationships in place the Horns were able to make the late addition. He was courted by the likes of Georgia and Oregon and was a one-time Colorado commit.

The player: Explosive outside athlete whether at receiver or cornerback. He'll play receiver but the fact he could play corner underscores his overall athleticism.

The skinny: He made a fair bit of noise this spring, particularly with his speed, and likely will again this August. Early returns are very good but he's still learning the playbook and finer points of the season.

Jordan Washington, TE, Houston (Texas) Langham Creek
On3 IR: 91.04, 4-star, No. 245

The recruitment: A&M tried but Washington was UT's to lose.

The player: Receiving ability jumps off the field but he also has the size and tenacity to become a quality in-line blocker. With some seasoning, Washington will be a legit two-way tight end.

The skinny: A theme is about to emerge in this article with players I find to be vastly underrated. Washington should have been a Top 100 player. The staff is very, very high on him after having the spring to coach him. He's one of the few true freshmen who should play real snaps this year.

Santana Wilson, CB, Scottsdale (Ariz) Desert Mountain
On3 IR: 91.00, 4-star, No. 250

The recruitment: No frills recruitment after Terry Joseph had some good ties into the family. Santana's father is Adrian Wilson, the former Arizona Cardinals standout safety.

The player: Wilson was one of only four players to not enroll early but that had more to do with it being difficult to graduate early in Arizona. He has very good football character, physicality, and explosiveness. He could play corner or nickel. If he does move to nickel, as with Jahdae Barron, it would not signal lack of cornerback athleticism.

The skinny: He could make a mark on coverage teams as a freshman.

Trey Owens, QB, Cypress (Texas) Cy-Fair
On3 IR: 90.68, 4-star, No. 275

The recruitment: Steve Sarkisian knew he wasn't going to land a high profile quarterback to follow Arch Manning. That doesn't mean they weren't going to land a very good one. Owens camped at Texas twice, including once when Arch was throwing, and won the staff over. It was Texas vs Texas.

The player: In the mold of the prototypical pocket passer at 6-foot-5, 230 pounds. Owens possesses a very strong arm and good mental traits.

The skinny: The book on him out of high school was he was composed and confident and that surely bore out during his first six months on campus. His spring game was about as impressive as you'll ever see for an early enrollee quarterback. Sark raves about Owens behind the scenes.

Daniel Cruz, C, North Richland Hills (Texas) Richland
On3 IR: 90.52, 4-star, No. 292

The recruitment: Ohio State and A&M were the main competition but nobody came close to prioritizing Cruz as much as Kyle Flood.

The player: The Vitruvian center. Cruz possesses tackle athleticism in a powerfully built guard body. Essentially, he has quickness for the run game and power to anchor in pass protection. Throw the ranking out, he's a future pro.

The skinny: He had a good spring but center isn't a position where you expect a true freshman to make an impact. He couldn't have a better mentor in Jake Majors. Don't be surprised if Cruz is starting in Year 2.

Christian Clark, RB, Phoenix (Ariz) Mountain Pointe
On3 IR: 90.06, 4-star, No. 336

The recruitment: Georgia and Oregon were the primary competitors. Tashard Choice put himself in excellent position with the Clarks before they ever set foot on campus. After the first unofficial visit this recruitment was essentially over.

The player: In high school he shared the workload with other talented running backs and was originally considered an athlete, though you could see he possessed running back nuances like vision, feet, balance, and lateral agility. Something else he possesses – long speed. It's my contention he has more upside than Gibson.

The skinny: Like Gibson, Clark has some intangibles that might get him on special teams early in his career.

Parker Livingstone, WR, Lucas (Texas) Lovejoy
On3 IR: 89.95, 4-star, No. 345

The recruitment: It was Texas for a very long time.

The player: I absolutely love this kid. He has size, ball skills, body control, and speed. He ran 21.69 200m as a sophomore. He knows how to find the end zone, too, after scoring 28 times between his sophomore and junior years. He was set to explode as a senior before a foot injury cost him his season.

The skinny: He's made some noise. He'll likely need the depth chart to thin a bit in front of him but he can ultimately become a 50-catch player.

Jordon Johnson-Rubell, S, Bradenton (Fla) IMG
On3 IR: 89.70, 4-star, No. 373

The recruitment: Johnson-Rubell originally being from Fort Worth gave Texas the inside track in this recruitment. Ohio State also gave chase.

The player: Smart, instinctive player with field general qualities for the middle of the field. JJ-R is a strong candidate for boundary safety in a year or two.

The skinny: One of the players mentioned by sources as having a good chance to find himself on special teams early in his career.

Tyanthony Smith, LB, Jasper (Texas)
On3 IR: 89.67, 4-star, No. 374

The recruitment: Texas played the long game and flipped Smith from A&M late in the process. He was a parting gift from former linebackers coach Jeff Choate.

The player: He's already put on 15 pounds of good weight. Weight and time to adapt to the college game is all he needs.

The skinny: Fast, physical player who knows how to find the ball carrier. Smith was also mentioned as a potential special-teamer for this year. Smith has NFL upside.

Alex January, DT, Duncanville (Texas)
On3 IR: 89.17, 3-star, No. 436

The recruitment: Florida State and LSU were the main competition but Texas had the inside track since his father, Michael, is a former Texas player.

The player: Here's a hard and fast rule: If the player is large, can move his feet, and will put forth just average effort he is a four-star. There are not a lot of Januarys walking around, especially when you see him up close. He is already well put together.

The skinny: He's one of the most important players in the program when you realize Texas is likely to lose five defensive tackles after this season. He should be ready for real snaps by his second season. He certainly flashed ability during the spring.

Freddie Dubose Jr., WR, Schertz (Texas) Smithson Valley
On3 IR: 89.17, 3-star, No. 439

The recruitment: Like with Livingstone, all it took for Texas to land him was to recruit him consistently.

The player: An outside, vertical receiving threat with good quickness and speed. He won bronze in the 400m after tearing his ACL his junior year.

The skinny: Similar to Butler in that he'll need some time to acclimate to the college game but when the roster thins out he should be ready to contribute.

Nate Kibble, IOL, Humble (Texas) Atascocita
On3 IR: 88.89, 3-star, No. 486

The recruitment: Kyle Flood didn't get the memo that Atascocita is a Texas A&M school.

The player: Not quite as athletic as DJ Campbell but similar with a wide base and long arms. Sharp young man.

The skinny: He'll need to wait his turn, and he's guard-specific, but he has a lot of quality traits and intangibles in his favor. He was not an early enrollee.

Melvin Hills, DL, Lafayette (La) Lafayette Christian Academy
On3 IR: 87.77, 3-star, No. 662

The recruitment: Ole Miss was the only other official visit he took.

The player: High motor player who projects to a number of alignments on the line. Will likely never be a sexy pass rusher but will do the dirty work.

The skinny: He'll need a year or two of time to develop. He was not an early enrollee.

Michael Kern, P, Fort Lauderdale (Fla) St. Thomas Aquinas
On3 IR: 80.51, 3-star, No. 2520

The recruitment: Texas needed a good punter in the class and got one.

The player: He punts.

The skinny: Steve Sarkisian and Jeff Banks didn't feel the need to get a punter in the portal due to Kern.

Thank You & Please Review

Thanks for reading the 12th annual Burnt Orange Bible. Please share it with your tribe, send the links to friends and family and write a 5 star review. Your readership and advocacy is vital in allowing us to create a great product and it can't continue without your support on social media and through your peer networks. Thanks for Thinking Texas Football with us and Hook 'em!

About the Authors/Creators

Paul Wadlington is a Texas graduate, author, podcaster, partner in a financial business and commercial real estate investor currently living in Colorado Springs, Colorado. You'll find his writing at Inside Texas and his chattering on The Everyone Gets A Trophy podcast. Feel free to reach out at trophymailbag@gmail.com

Will Gallagher is a supremely talented professional photographer, Austin native and Texas graduate whose work can be found at http://gallagherstudios.com. He has been with Inside Texas since 2003. Will provided the incredible photos that enrich this book.

Eric Nahlin is a recruiting industry expert, Longhorn insider, and the managing partner at Inside Texas. He lives in Houston...if you define Houston by the endless suburbs and small towns that border the actual city, which is how everyone defines it.

Made in the USA
Coppell, TX
21 July 2024

35027330R00090